THE WONDERFUL WANDERERS

BOLTON WANDERERS 1874 TO 1960

THE WONDERFUL WANDERERS

BOLTON WANDERERS 1874 TO 1960

JEFF WILLIAMSON

First Publishied in Great Britain in 2015 by DB Publishing, an imprint of JMD Media Ltd

ISBN 978-1-78091-530-2

Printed and bound in the UK by Copytech (UK) Ltd Peterborough

PREFACE

Britain has changed immeasurably since the formation of the Football Association on 26 October, 1863, football became our national game and like the British Empire we led the world in it and most other things. We then moved into the twentieth century in a similar position, but the shift in world dominance was changing. The great game went through two world wars and a crippling depression from the late 1920s, which had still not concluded in 1940 when we were already at war with Germany. It survived all this and was a great morale booster for the country and its people. It has gone from strength to strength and moved swiftly with the times. It is said that Britain as a nation changed even more rapidly morally and culturally during the 1960s and the same can be said of football and most certainly Bolton Wanderers are included in that.

Today we have a completely different way of life, more often than not for the better, though we should not be blind or too quick to dismiss the past, as there is a great deal we can learn from it by embracing it and drawing on the brilliance of the Wanderers from those bygone times.

CONTENTS

9 Foreword

11 Introduction

16 The Beginning and Background

29 Club success 1885–1920

54 Tributes to the fallen 1914–18

57 Club Success 1920–39

69 War years and War Cup 1939–45

73 War Cup 1944–45 players

82 Walter Sidebottom –
Tribute to the loss of a brave and gifted young player

86 Club Success 1946–58

96 Players from the 1953 FA Cup Final

100 Players from the 1958 FA Cup Final and Charity Shield

109 The Special Ones – 1920s Wonderful Wanderers

131 The Dedicated Trainer

133 Bolton Wanderers: Tour results up to 1940.

136 Introduction to a Legend

138 Nathaniel 'Nat' Lofthouse: The Man–The Legend. (Our Lofty)

155 Other players with Lancashire Cup Winning honours

176 Other players with Lancashire Cup final Runner Up medals

180 Other early Bolton players with representative honours during their career

185 Conclusions and Views

186 Post 1960 honours

188 Thanks and Dedications

FOREWORD

by John Ritson

It is an honour to be given the opportunity to pen my thoughts about Bolton Wanderers and my time there. I signed for Bolton in 1965 as a 16-year-old apprentice professional. It was a big decision to make but one that turned out to be the best one I ever made.

Within a few months I was playing at Bolton's training ground in Bromwich Street with the Brazilian football team and Pele. They had decided to use our facilities to prepare for their defence of the World Cup 1966 in England, as they were based in the North West. That in itself was an experience of a lifetime.

I then played my way through the Bolton B, A and reserve sides under the guidance of manager Bill Ridding, respected coach George Taylor and trainer George Hunt. I finally broke into the first team and made by debut at West Bromwich Albion. About this time I had also been selected for the England Under-21's at Aston Villa, but on arrival I was summoned back to Birmingham to go with the first team for a cup game at West Ham, which we ended up losing 4–1, so mixed feelings there.

Over the next few years we went through a transitional period with several different managers. I played with many of the players mentioned in the book such as Eddie Hopkinson, Brian Edwards, Roy Hartle, Francis Lee and Freddie Hill. Players with great experience and skill, who passed on their knowledge to me. Our fortunes then turned in the mid-seventies under the guidance of Ian Greaves and his assistant George Mulhall. We strengthened our squad with players like Sam Allardyce, Peter Reid, Paul Jones and Garry Jones mixed with the experience of Roy Greaves, Tony Dunne, Willy Morgan, Frank Worthington and myself. The magic of Greaves and Mulhall worked wonders and we won promotion into the First Division now the Premier League, in 1977–78. I have to add that in my opinion Ian Greaves was the best league manager of that period.

You can then imagine my disappointment the following season when contract terms did not go my way and I ended up moving to Bury FC under former Bolton player Dave Hatton, who was soon to leave. Again things did not go to plan and I decided to hang up my boots as they say. It was the hardest decision I ever made after 14 great years at Bolton Wanderers, but after gaining success with them and eventually captaining the club, I felt I had achieved my boyhood ambition.

I met Ian Greaves and George Mulhall along with some ex-colleagues at Nat Lofthouse's funeral in 2011, Ian told me that letting me go was the worst decision he ever made, which is good to know but still leaves you with those nagging thoughts of what might have been.

I am proud to have played for such an historical and influential club as Bolton and was lucky enough to know, play and have as friends some of their greats of the past. Nat Lofthouse the epitome of Bolton Wanderers was still with the club when I was there so I got to know him very well; I also played under him when he briefly managed the club. I can assure you that everything written or said about him is true, a great man.

All in all a marvellous family orientated club, with a great spirit and Burnden Park a football ground that has given me many treasured memories. Bolton Wanderers have without doubt made their mark in football history.

INTRODUCTION

'THE WONDERFUL WANDERERS'

This book is inspired by my obsession and love of Bolton Wanderers and hopefully to make more people aware of just how good they really were, the effect they have had on peoples lives and especially mine, both on and off the pitch. All my family from as far back as my parents can recall have been loyal followers of The Trotters. I can say without hesitation because of this influence on my family, they have shaped how I have lived my football-obsessed life. It is, I would say, a type of religion and regardless of the team's position, something I don't think I ever want to be without. It's a family club, which dependent on their form, also seems to strangely affect the mood of the town in a similar manner. I was born in the Bolton area at Townleys Hospital off Plodder Lane in 1956, it is now known simply as Bolton General Hospital. This is the area where Bolton's first ever venture into the football world took place and from boy to man any football talk in my family has always centred round them. I don't want to bore you with my whole life, but to explain in brief why I am Wanderers through and through, does add some clarity as to how and why I will always follow them and hopefully encourage others to do the same.

GROUND CALL

BOLTON WANDERERS F.C.
BURNDEN PARK, BOLTON,
LANCASHIRE

From the stories my Father and Mother were told by their parents of watching the famous teams up to and beyond the 1920s, the Wembley triumph in 1923, right through to their own experiences into the 1960s. This followed on with my first encounter at Burnden Park and the men in white and blue in 1965. There was the Saturday or midweek ritual of parking the car on Manchester

Road, walking down with my father past the greyhound stadium and on to the large concrete car park in front of the ground. As a child it just looked so imposing, but it was an amazing rush of adrenalin every time and always gave me butterflies in my stomach, which I can still remember to this day. To me they were world-beaters and I could not wait to get into the ground to watch them play.

My Aunt, Elsie Williamson and my mother worked for the club from the early 1950s and were ardent followers from the mid 1940s. We used to meet them outside the main entrance by the supporters club pre match to get the early team news and if that wasn't good enough, I was also occasionally allowed into the main clubhouse for a look around. My god how lucky was I as a kid strolling around a place I perceived as the equivalent of heaven? Topping off the adventure with then being allowed to stand in the player's tunnel and watch them go out onto the pitch; I can still hear the thunderous sound of studs clattering past me. I do recall my Aunt introducing me to Nat Lofthouse for the first time as a nervous 9-year-old, he had that mild calming Lancashire accent and after a few words he just smiled and patted me on the head. I was totally dumbstruck and unable to formulate any kind of response beyond words of one syllable. If that was now I would probably never wash my hair again. Elsie and my parents got to know Nat really well, they said he was the friendliest, most down to earth person you could wish to meet with time for everyone not just football fans and every person I meet who met him says the same thing.

At one point I had three Aunts and my mother working at the club and my father was contracted to decorate some of the player's houses, so we always seemed to be connected in the day–to-day running of the club in one way or another. Elsie was dedicated to Bolton and worked there until 1973 when she was given a special presentation on her retirement, which was attended by some of the players including Nat Lofthouse. My cousin then took up that role for several more years into the early 1980s. After her retirement Elsie married newspaper reporter Bill Clarke after his first

wife had died, Bill worked for the Mirror group. He was in fact the brother of Alf Clarke himself a talented sports reporter and writer. Alf had been personally retained by Manchester United and was a favourite of Matt Busby. He had been a junior player at the club before turning to journalism and was a fanatical fan of the Red Devils. He wrote a now sought-after book on them in the 1950s, though he was tragically killed in the Munich air disaster of 1958. I treasure my copy of his book, which is pictured with his image.

Bolton as a family club and always looked after their own, it still applies today but not I feel in the same intimate way, time seem to have changed that. My Aunt was a complete football fanatic who adored Bolton Wanderers and Nat Lofthouse

Nat Lofthouse centre, to his right is my Dad then Elsie and my Mum. To Nat's left is fellow work colleague and good friend Alice Gregory, back left of the photograph is Bert Gregory. Front right is Mr Partridge, club scout. They are at a Christmas dinner around 1956. (They made sure Nat got home safely on Mr Ridding's instructions!)

Another Christmas function in the 1950s at Aspin Hall, Bolton. Bert and Alice are sat front with Bolton Chairman Mr Duxbury, seated and behind him is another board member Mr Hayward. My Mum, Elsie and Dad are centre behind Alice and Bert.

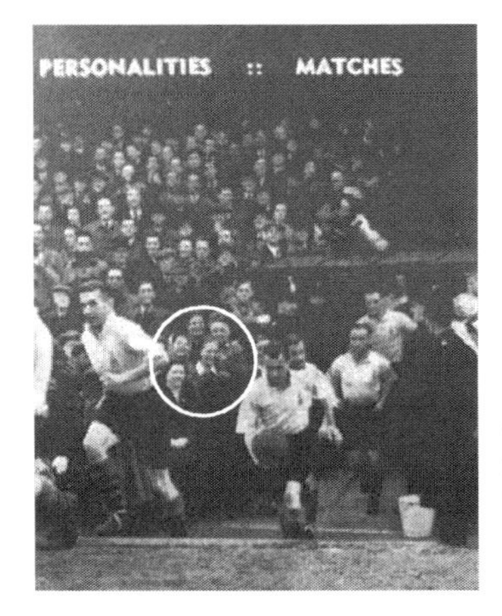

Above left is a 1950 magazine about the club. Circled are my Mum and Elsie as the players go onto the pitch before the game. They are also right in a similar scene again pre match 1948.

in particular; her whole life was centred round family and football, she always said she had two families. There was never a bad word that could be spoken about Lofthouse, or any member of the team for that matter and woe betide the man that did. I was subconsciously indoctrinated into that Bolton Wanderers way of life and it is only as I got older and started to research the club that I realised I have always been surrounded by them. They did literally mean everything to my family, so it really is no surprise that I am possessed of the same values and beliefs. I can find myself talking to literally anybody even a complete stranger, sometimes quite passionately about Bolton Wanderers.

As a football club their impact on the game is immeasurable since they were formed and over the years I have collected a large amount of memorabilia and facts on them, making me even more obsessed about their past. This is why I put pen to paper to share with others their exploits as a football club and specifically in the art of winning cups.

We will now move on to how Bolton began, though not in the complete detailed factual sense, as the main body of this information on Bolton Wanderers has been told many times before. I do feel it is necessary in some way to paint the picture that leads onto the teams that had so many successes in Cup football. Some people will not be aware of many of these achievements, which makes the telling even more of a necessity. What will become apparent are their many triumphs from the 1800s through to the late 1950s and their part as one of the main clubs that became the driving force in creating the Football League we know and have today. This was under the guidance of men like J.J. Bentley, one of the clubs early and more high-profile managers, later a board member. He also worked with Manchester United and had a huge influence on football when he was appointed to the committee of the Football Association.

The Wanderers are steeped in history and have had some great moments, widely written about and highly respected in football terms and a lot of this history still resonates to this day.

THE BEGINNING AND BACKGROUND

They were formed in the towns hard, but somewhat prosperous working class mill environment in 1874, as Christ Church FC by Rev John Farrell Wright and the master of the school attached to the church on Deane Road, Thomas Ogden. Ogden formed a partnership with Wright for the betterment of the school and people of the town. They formed the football team after examining the way the Turton football club was run. Turton had been established in 1871 by the prominent Kay family and was the first in Lancashire to do so with J.J. Bentley among their numbers, who was himself a good player who also represented Lancashire. Ogden would captain the side playing football matches at the Dick Cockle recreation playing fields in Deane, with the permission of the church, which is

Christ Church, Deane Road circa 1886. It was demolished in 1936. Rev Wright had previously been at St Peter's, which is now Bolton Parish Church; Deane Road was formerly Blackburn Street. The site then formed part of Christ Church Gardens and a car park.

The recreation field and changing rooms were opposite the Cross Guns Public House, where they also held their club meetings. The fields are now housing estates.

The Vicar of Christ Church and researcher Mrs Page are seen at the site of Wright's grave. He died in 1883.

pictured, but no longer in existence. The joining fee was sixpence in old money and then a penny a week.

Reverend Wright and Thomas Ogden's resting places were traced after many years in 2008, by researcher Peter Lupson. Wright is buried at Christ Church, Walmsley and Ogden in Heaton Cemetery, Bolton. After a number of disagreements in 1877 with the church and Reverend Wright in particular, who they believed exerted too much control over proceedings, the club 'wandered' as it was put, to the Gladstone Hotel, Deane, which is pictured below to the left of the large building. Bolton Wanderers were formed here on 28 August, 1877. The buildings were demolished in 1965.

They then acquired use of land at Pikes Lane, Deane. This was to become their home ground until the move to Burnden Park in 1895. Pikes lane left, is now also a housing estate.

The committee and members would now regularly meet at the pictured Britannia Hotel, Derby Street, Deane. (Premises were demolished in 1965.)

The Wanderers began to gather a sound reputation under the long-term guidance and helpful patronage of local mill owner and businessman Peter Parkinson, quickly becoming a popular and respected club nationally. The team is pictured here in 1882–83 and this is one of the earliest known photographs. They had just won the Bolton Charity Cup in May 1883, 3–0 against Gilnow Rangers. They had also won this competition the previous season 6–1 in a replay against Astley Bridge. In 1884–85 they secured this competition again beating Great Lever 5–1 on 9 May, 1885.

In 1888 they became a founder member of the football league. The handwritten result season sheet of the original teams and their form in this first league season is pictured (see page 31).

Bolton Wanderers until the early 1960s competed at the highest level and had a considerable reputation within football circles. They were a major force in English football and one of the main competing top sides. They have always produced home talent and had a good scouting and youth system. They were one of the first clubs known for producing players from within the ranks and had excellent training methods. Money always an issue, had to be spent wisely and they did spend to progress,

This is believed to be the oldest team picture taken of the Wanderers in the 1882-83 season. On the back row, from left, were J. Kenneth, G. Dobson, A Bromley, J McKernan, W. Steele, and umpire J. Parkinson. Front row: T. Howarth, J. Fallon, W. Struthers, J. Gleaves (captain), K. Devonport, J. Scholes. They had just won the Bolton Charity Cup.

even in the early days. As time ticked by this continued, examples like Dick Pym bought for £5,000 was a then record for a 'keeper, but this put the club in some difficulties in the early 1920s. David Jack another purchase and the most sought after player at this time, by the mid 1920s, he was later sold to Arsenal for a then world record fee of £10,890, double the previous record. This then funded the finances of the club that were still suffering and this strangely all took place in perhaps Bolton's best ever decade in football. They were performing at the highest level in what could be argued world football and fans did query at times where all the money was going. In the main though due to the clubs reputation, they usually managed to keep most of their best players, as well as bringing in quality replacements, unlike today. Nat Lofthouse once stated; "If I had been playing in the modern game, I would have struggled to stay at one club". Then as we moved further through time into the sixties and beyond, fans persistently complained that we could no longer hold onto our quality players and this theme unfortunately still seems to continue into the present day.

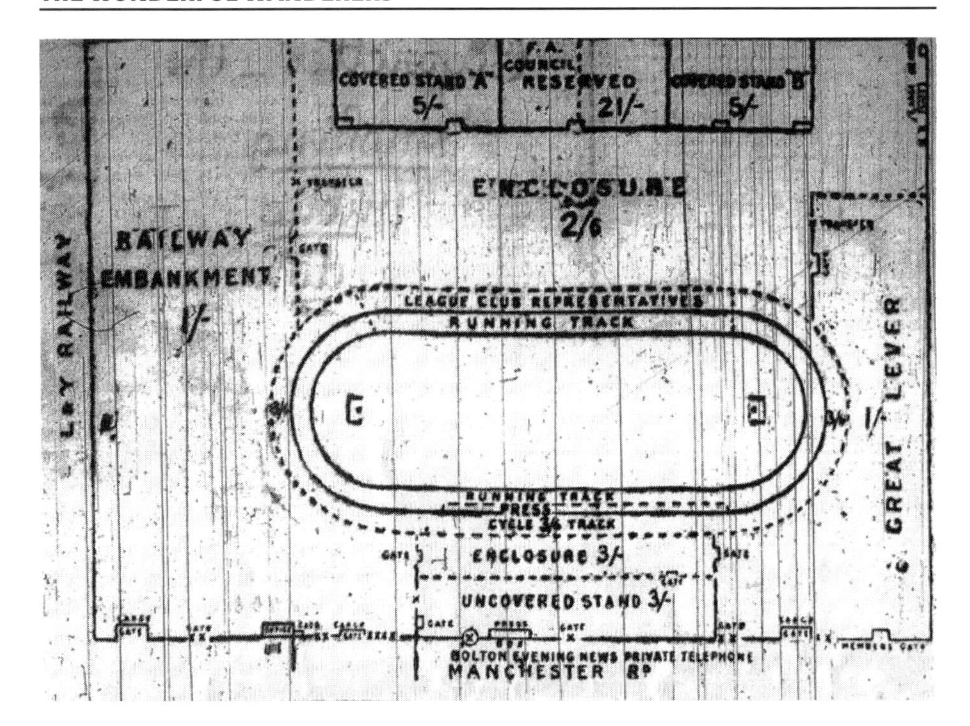

When Burnden Park became their fortress from 1895 for the initial yearly fee of £130 on a fourteen year lease, it was a place visiting teams feared as the

tough but quality teams that were being churned out showed and have no doubt, quality players wanted to play for Bolton Wanderers.

It was the only ground in the country that was raised on a platform style base and was used for many other matches including FA Cup Final replays and as a semi-final venue. A ground held in high regard by the Football Association. The official record crowd in 1933 was 69,912 for a match against Manchester City. The statistics state the capacity was 70,000. (Pictured 1940s)

In the Burnden disaster of 1946 they believe that over 80,000 plus were packed in for the FA Cup tie against Stoke City with Stanley Matthews playing. This picture shows the awful consequences of the tragedy in which 33 people died and around 500 were injured. A plaque originally at Burnden Park is now again in place outside the Macron Stadium in tribute to those who died.

Sadly the ground fell into disrepair from the 1970s onward and after crowd control was rigorously introduced. With lack of finances, part of the embankment end was sold for the building of the Normid superstore, which offensively protruded into this large stand. This was after the teams slide into the lower divisions in the 1980s and was probably the lowest point in the clubs football history. The stadium was quite unsightly on the eye and apparently too costly for re-development. This hastened the reason for selling and moving to the Reebok Stadium, which is a magnificent looking complex, situated on the Middlebrook retail park in Horwich. This ground is not geared for the attendances of the past, with the capacity being under 30,000. The question was I suppose, could Bolton still attract the large crowds needed to finance the team and a much larger stadium?

(The Reebok changed in the 2014–15 season to the Macron Stadium due to a new sponsorship deal.)

Burnden Park closed its gates on 25 April, 1997 after a 4–1 defeat of Charlton Athletic. In a repeating theme as seen with the previously mentioned landmarks associated with Bolton Wanderers past, it was demolished in 1999 after falling into a terrible and forgotten state. The shadows of history that once fell across Burnden Park was now gone forever.

To have been able to bring a football enthusiast to this ground, if re-development had been possible to let them see and feel the history it held would have been a tremendous thrill. For me the place simply dripped with atmosphere and you could almost smell the history around you. Now it's just a memory only seen through old footage and pictures, it's such a tragedy. This area is now the site of an Asda and other retail stores, which still fills me with nostalgia every time I pass it.

We cannot bring it back, but we can look at the great Bolton Wanderers triumphs from 1883, which set the benchmark for future teams to emulate right through to the late 1950s and beyond, many of them at Burnden. Their FA and other Cup victories are legendary. This was in an era when trophies such as the Lancashire and Manchester Cup (nine wins) were as revered and as hard fought for as the FA Cup. The Lancashire Cup being the oldest competition in English football and was a highly prized trophy; we therefore give this some extra attention. In the late 1800s through to the mid 1900s it seemed to hold as much importance as the FA Cup, but the growth of that competition eventually overtook it.

Other cups coming into their possession were as stated the Bolton Charity Cup (six times), Derbyshire Cup, Richardson Cup (twice) and West Lancashire Cup (twice), all tough competitions, which today do not hold the same prestige. In the Lancashire Cup Bolton have most appearances at the time of press, 114, with 12 wins (one shared) and nine further final appearances only bettered by Manchester United and Blackburn Rovers. The clubs best sides generally contested these competitions; they wanted to win the cups. This makes the club name on these trophies even more important and prestigious during the eras in question.

For some of the earlier players their time at the club was a pioneering one and an example for others to try and emulate. It helped forge and cement the image and structure of Bolton Wanderers in becoming one of the UK's best known teams. These men were involved in their Cup winning exploits and also establishing Bolton as a top tier side. They may now be long gone, but should not be forgotten as Bolton Wanderers would not be the club it is today without their services.

The first players who were recorded and registered with the club are listed in the 1880 records: Wilson (Goalkeeper). Naylor and Bradley (full-backs); Gleaves, Evans (half-backs); Sharples, Naylor (left-wing); Baybutt, Bailey (centres). Other's listed where Blackhurst, Bradley, Horridge, Morrison, Parkinson, Waddington, Bowker, Crawford, Fletcher, Parkinson, E. Fletcher. They were by all reports a very tough group of players, but as Percy Young describes in his history of Bolton Wanderers they had an Achilles heel. A match against Turton by the second team in December, 1880 was abandoned; why, because it started to rain!

The first recorded team photo shown earlier with the Bolton Charity Cup has only two of the above listed players in it, so the club was moving forward with some pace. A number of players made their mark with Bolton and also gained other representative honours; Tom Naylor for example was a founder member of the club and a talented full-back. He was the first Bolton player to represent Lancashire on 27 November, 1880 against North Wales. He was described by the *Manchester Guardian* as a tower of strength to the club.

Players from 1882–83 team photo:

J. Kennedy. From the Church area of East Lancashire and initially played for Darwen. He was a half-back first mentioned in 1881, was still playing in 1885 and is listed as playing 10 recorded games for Bolton. He is known to have represented Lancashire on at least one occasion against Cleveland, in a 5–4 victory in 1883. He won the Bolton Charity Cup with Bolton.

George Dobson. Born in Bolton and played for Bolton until the end of the 1884 season. He was spotted by Everton in a home game against Bolton at their new Walton Breck Road ground, Liverpool on 24 November, 1884. The game ended in a 2–2 draw, which Everton were happy with until they found out Bolton had sent their second eleven. He then signed for Everton as one of their first full-time professionals, playing for them till after 1888. He also represented the Lancashire select side when he was still a Bolton player and was a member of the successful Bolton Charity Cup side.

James McKernan was born in Scotland and was signed from Hibernian in 1882 after playing against Bolton in a friendly match, which Hibs won 3–0 in 1881, playing for them as an amateur. He was then in their side that played again at Pikes Lane in 1882. He had already won the Edinburgh Association Cup with them. An impressive full-back and described as a strong defensive asset. He was feared by visiting teams for his presence and formed part of a tough back line with Jim Powell, Kennedy and Bob Roberts. He has 17 recorded games for Bolton and took over the captaincy from James Gleaves in 1884. Because of his amateur status he worked in the aforementioned Britannia Inn, Bolton to earn a reasonable living, which the FA frowned upon as it was licenced premises. He was still listed in archive match reports as playing for the Wanderers in 1887 and was with the club when they won the Lancashire, Derbyshire and Bolton Charity cups. He was also a runner up in the Lancashire Cup in 1886–87.

William 'Billy' Steele. Another tough Scot coming to Wanderers from Arbroath in 1880–01, he was recommended by fellow Scot James Devlin who had earlier played for Bolton after answering a newspaper advertisement, but lost an eye in a mill accident and had to retire from the game. Steele was a half-back who could play on either side and also at centre-half. He is listed with eight recorded games for Bolton, though he is still listed in the team in other 1888 fixtures. It is also believed he was paid £1–£2 per week for his services, which the Scottish FA would have banned him for. He won the Lancashire and Derbyshire Cups, as well as the Charity Cup with Bolton in 1885. He was also a runner up in the Lancashire Cup in 1886–87.

Tom Howarth and P. Howarth. Both pre-league players. There is a Howarth listed in the Charity Cup side and the squad when the team won the Lancashire Cup in 1885–86 and again playing in the Final the following year, losing 3–0 against Preston at Pikes Lane. Though whether one in the same played in both matches is not recorded. The available listed records show Tom with six games and one goal for the club, plus another one in the 1884 friendly game against Hearts at Pikes Lane. He broke his leg in 1884 and was allowed a benefit game in the same year. P. Howarth had eight games and three goals. (His 1886–87 Lancashire Cup runner up medal went to auction in 2013), so in all likelihood it was probably him that played due to the injury to Tom Howarth.

L. Fallon. He was a local player registered from around 1882 who is shown with six games and five goals as an inside-forward or half-back. He won the Charity, Derby and Lancashire Cups with the club in 1885. He represented the Lancashire select side in 1883 against Ayrshire. He is also shown with credit for one goal in a 4–0 thrashing of Hearts in a friendly at Pikes Lane in 1884 before a 6,000 crowd. He was in the side until after 1886.

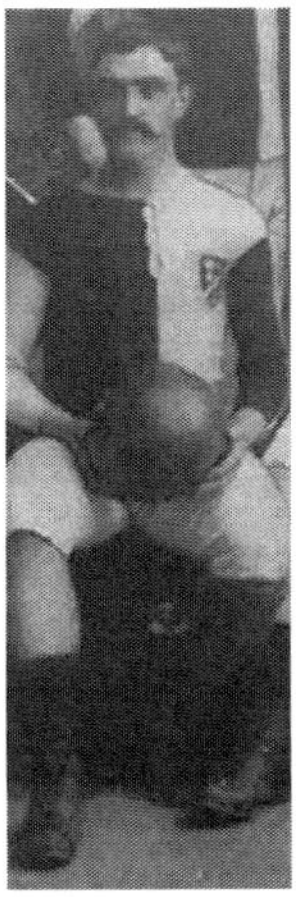

William Giffen Struthers. He was initially at Partick Thistle then was a Glasgow Rangers player, part of 'The Gallant Pioneers' who were instrumental in the establishment of Rangers becoming a major force in Scotland. He was part of the Rangers team that won the Glasgow Merchant Cup in 1879, scoring the goal that won the game. He then came to Bolton in 1880, again in answer to a newspaper advertisement asking for players, as many of Bolton's other Scottish based players had done. A centre-forward described in the press as 'splendidly built, with beguiling skill in the art of dribbling and ball control that perplexed the English player'. He knew the game and could motivate other team members to better their involvement and performance, which was also reported as a joy to watch. He was a superb marksman and in 19 recorded games scored 18 goals.

He was instrumental in capturing the Lancashire Cup in 1885 and was a runner up in the same competition the following season. He also secured medals for the Bolton Charity and Derbyshire Cups.

In 1886 when nearing the end of his career and was caught up in the internal wrangling's of the club. He was elected Secretary, more by pressure due to his seniority as a player and took the position with some discomfort. He did not suit the position and disliked the role. Fitzroy Norris replaced him in 1887. He too was unsuccessful and the famous J.J. Bentley took up the mantle again after his removal the previous year and normality was resumed.

James Gleaves. A local player who captained the team after joining in 1880 until 1884, he was a half-back listed with 13 games and two goals and represented Lancashire in 1883. He won the Charity Cup and is holding the trophy in the 1882–83 team photograph.

Kenny Davenport. He was born on 23 March, 1862 and died on 29 September, 1908 age 46 years. He is listed on his death certificate as a beerseller.

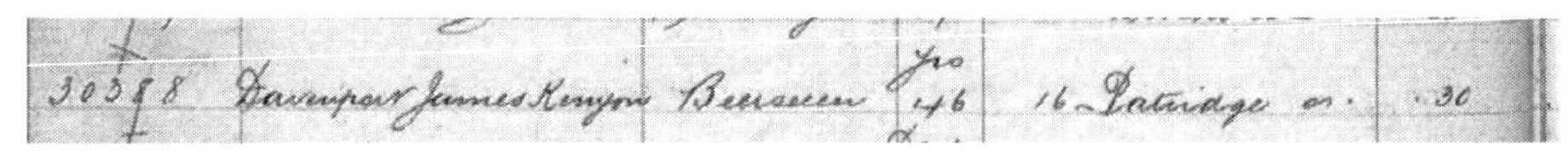

Davenport James Kenyon | Beerseller | 46 | 16 Partridge St. | 30

He was from Deane and signed for Bolton from local club Gilnow Rangers in 1883 as an inside-forward, but he could also play on the wing. He was Bolton's first England International in 1885, playing against Wales and gained two caps in total. There is controversy over his goals, he has two recorded, but a lot of the goals in those days were scrimmage goalmouth affairs when it was difficult to see if someone was kicking the ball or the player. Some records credit his goals to Fred Geary in a 9–1 drubbing of

Bolton 1889: Back row players: Robinson, Parkinson, Jones, Roberts. J.J. Bentley, Manager is back right. Middle: Davenport, Brogan, Cassidy, McNee, Weir. Front: Milne, Bullough.

Ireland in Belfast. He also represented Lancashire on a number of occasions and was highly thought of. He is famously credited after much deliberation with the first ever recorded league goal against Derby County at Pikes Lane on 8 September, 1888. He scored two on the day, but Bolton lost 6–3 after leading 3–0.

He played 77 games and scored 36 goals for Bolton and was given a benefit year in 1889. He won the Lancashire Cup in 1885–56 and was also a runner up in the same competition. He also won the Bolton Charity and Derbyshire Cups. He joined Southport Central in 1892, then retired and returned to the Wanderers in a training capacity, assisting with the reserve side. He is credited with scouting George Kay who signed for Bolton from Eccles. He described Kay as 'as strong a lad as I have ever seen, big and fast'. Kay later transferred to West Ham and captained them in the 1923 FA Cup Final, ironically against Bolton. Kay was instrumental in Liverpool's rise to success when manager from 1936 to 1951, winning the First Division in 1947. Kay introduced Bill Paisley and Billy Liddell to the Liverpool ranks. Davenport is buried in Heaton Cemetery on Gilnow Road, Bolton.

J. Scholes: Little is known of him other than being listed with 2 games and 1 goal.

As we progress into the clubs successes we detail mainly the records of the games, teams and the players involved. Hopefully you will be able to transport yourself into their world and at least momentarily relive the glory they shared. If you love football history, as a football fan you have got to admire the achievements of Bolton, even more so if you are a Wanderers follower.

Right up to the late 1960s and into the 1970s many teams could compete on an even keel. There were always the stronger sides, though money was not the major contributory factor to success, a lot of teams had the opportunity to make their mark and did so, as records show.

CLUB SUCCESSES 1885 TO 1920:

1. 1885–6. Lancashire Cup winners. This was the first year Bolton won this highly sought after and oldest trophy in the English game, first played for in 1879–80. This same year they won the Bolton Charity and Derbyshire Cups, which are displayed in the team photo. They beat Derby County 2–0 for the Derbyshire Cup and Halliwell 4–1 for the Bolton Charity Cup.

They played Blackburn Rovers in the Lancashire Final beating Burnley Wanderers 7–0, South Shore 3–0, Blackburn Olympic 11–2, Blackpool St Johns 9–1 and Darwen 2–1 to get there. At that time Blackburn were one of the top teams in the country, who had already won this competition four times. The game was played at Deepdale, Preston on 17 April, 1886 in front of 7,000 fans. Bolton came out on top by 1–0 with the only goal coming from J. Hewitson the left-winger, pictured front second from right in the 1885 team photo.

Blackburn Rovers have won the Lancashire Cup 18 times in total.

Lancashire Cup Final team: Trainer, Holden, Parkinson, Steele, Davenport, Bullough, Brogan, Fallon, Struthers, Hough, Hewitson.

1886–87: Runners up to Preston 3–0 in Lancashire Cup.
1887–88: Bolton again secured the Bolton Charity Cup in June, 1888 beating Farnworth Standard 5–1.
1888–89: Bolton reached the FA Cup semi-final, but lost at the Perry Barr ground, Birmingham to Sheffield Wednesday 2–1, before 15,000, our scorer was McNee. Bolton had beaten Distillery 10–2, then Sheffield United 13–0 still the record win to date, Joe Cassidy netting five. They then beat Preston 3–2.
First Football League Year: The first year of the league was completed and the sheet below shows a review of the season, they finished fifth. Bolton also retained the Charity Cup in May 1890 with a 3–2 victory against Heywood Central. This seems to be the last recorded year for the Wanderers in this competition.

The Football League 1888 · 1889 (Alphabetically Arranged.) — Results of 132 Matches

Position	Club	Accrington	Aston Villa	B'burn Rovers	Bolton Wanderers	Burnley	Derby County	Everton	Notts County	Preston N.E.	Stoke	West Brom. Albion	Wolverhampton Wanderers	No. of Matches 22 Each: Won	Lost	Drawn		Goals: For	Against	Points	Position
7	Accrington	. . / . .	34 / 11	55 / 02	14 / 23	51 / 22	11 / 62	12 / 31	33 / 12	00 / 02	42 / 20	23 / 21	44 / 04	6	8	8		48	48	20	7
2	Aston Villa	43 / 11	. . / . .	61 / 15	32 / 62	42 / 04	42 / 25	21 / 01	91 / 42	11 / 02	51 / 11	20 / 33	11 / 21	12	5	5		61	43	29	2
4	B'burn Rovers	55 / 20	16 / 51	. . / . .	44 / 23	71 / 42	20 / 30	30 / 13	33 / 52	01 / 22	52 / 12	62 / 12	22 / 22	10	6	6		66	45	26	4
5	Bolton Wanderers	41 / 32	23 / 26	44 / 32	. . / . .	34 / 14	36 / 32	62 / 12	40 / 73	13 / 25	21 / 22	51 / 12	23 / 21	10	10	2		63	59	22	5
9	Burnley	15 / 22	24 / 40	17 / 24	43 / 41	. . / . .	10 / 01	22 / 23	16 / 10	25 / 22	34 / 21	34 / 20	14 / 04	7	12	3		42	62	17	9
10	Derby County	11 / 26	24 / 52	02 / 03	63 / 23	01 / 10	. . / . .	24 / 26	32 / 52	23 / 05	21 / 11	12 / 05	14 / 30	7	13	2		41	60	16	10
8	Everton	21 / 13	12 / 20	03 / 31	26 / 21	22 / 32	42 / 62	. . / . .	21 / 12	03 / 02	00 / 21	14 / 01	05 / 12	9	11	2		35	47	20	8
11	Notts County	33 / 21	19 / 24	33 / 25	04 / 37	61 / 01	23 / 25	12 / 31	. . / . .	07 / 14	03 / 03	24 / 21	30 / 12	5	15	2		39	73	12	11
1	Preston N.E.	00 / 20	41 / [illegible]	10 / [illegible]	31 / 52	52 / 22	33 / 50	10 / 20	70 / 41	. . / . .	70 / 30	30 / 50	40 / 52	18	.	4		74	15	40	1
12	Stoke	24 / 02	16 / 11	25 / 21	12 / 23	43 / 12	32 / 11	00 / 12	30 / 30	07 / 03	. . / . .	02 / 02	01 / 14	4	14	4		26	51	12	12
6	West Brom. Albion	22 / 12	02 / 33	26 / 21	15 / 21	43 / 02	21 / 50	41 / 10	42 / 12	03 / 05	20 / 20	. . / . .	12 / 13	10	10	2		40	46	22	6
3	Wolverhampton Wanderers	44 / 40	11 / 12	22 / 22	32 / 12	41 / 40	41 / 03	50 / 21	03 / 21	04 / 25	10 / 41	21 / 31	. . / . .	12	6	4		51	37	28	3
	Goals For	48	61	66	63	42	41	35	39	74	26	40	51	110	110	44		586	586	264	
	Goals Against	48	43	45	59	62	60	47	73	15	51	46	37	April 1889. R.H. Richards.							

(1) North End. (2) Aston Villa (3) Wolv'hampton Wand. (4) B'burn Rovers (5) Bolton Wand. (6) West Brom. (7) Accrington (8) Everton (9) Burnley (10) Derby Cty (11) Notts Cty (12) Stoke.

2. 1890–91. Lancashire Cup winners. Opponents were Darwen, the first ever winners. To get there they beat Higher Walton 2–1, Everton 6–0 and Blackburn R. 2–0. The Final was played at Anfield on 25 April, 1891. Attendance 7,000. The result in Bolton's favour was 3–1 with goals from Jones, Brogan and Cassidy.

The team was: Sutcliffe, Somerville, Jones, Paton, Gardiner, Roberts, Munro, Brogan, Cassidy, McNee, Turner.

In 1891–92 season Bolton achieved the first of their highest Division One league finishes, third. The following season they were beaten finalists in the Lancashire Cup, a 2–0 defeat by Preston. Bolton regularly competed against Blackburn and Preston around this era and they were considered as the country's best two sides, yet Bolton more than held their own against them both.

Darwen have just one Lancashire Cup win, the first competition in 1879–80.

1893–94 Players only. Back: McArthur, Cassidy, Paton, Turner. Middle: Gardiner, Sutcliffe, Sommerville, Weir, Bentley, Front: Tannahill, Ferguson.

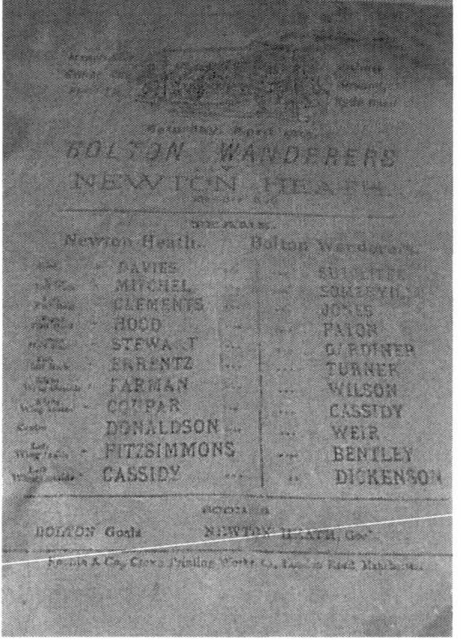

BOLTON WANDERERS
NEWTON HEATH

Newton Heath	Bolton Wanderers
DAVIES	[illegible]
MITCHEL	[illegible]
CLEMENTS	JONES
HOOD	PATON
STEWART	GARDINER
ERRENTZ	TURNER
FARMAN	WILSON
COUPAR	CASSIDY
DONALDSON	WEIR
FITZSIMMONS	BENTLEY
CASSIDY	DICKENSON

BOLTON Goals NEWTON HEATH, Goals

Pictured is the programme sheet from the April 1893 Manchester Cup Final, unfortunately resulting in a 2–1 defeat. The Newton Heath team later to reform as Manchester United is pictured; they had also beaten Bolton in the Final the previous year.

(Note: During this time prior to the formation of the Football League there were many unrecorded arranged games, so it is highly likely that team members played a lot more games with more goals than are actually known. There were also the cup competitions such as the Lancashire Cup, Bolton Charity Cup, Derbyshire Cup and later the Manchester Cup, which would give some of them even better statistics. The recorded details in this book are from research and are not definitive.)

An early Newton Heath team group believed to be from the season 1892-93.
Back row: Henrys, Clements. Middle row: Timmons (Trainer), Coupar, Perrins, Stewart, Errentz, Mitchell. Front row: Farman, Hood, Donaldson, Fitzsimmons, Colville.

1894–55 team players only Back: McGuigan, Sommerville, Sutcliffe, Jones. Middle: Tannahill, Paton, Freebairn, Cassidy. Front: Brown, Joyce, Wright.

3. 1893–94 season FA Cup Finalists. That year the team finished, thirteenth in Division 1. They lost in the Final of the Lancashire Cup 2–1 to Everton at Hyde Road, Manchester and were semi-finalists in the Manchester Cup going out against Heywood Central 2–1 at Gigg Lane, Bury.

The FA Cup Final was played at Goodison Park (see sketch page 41), Everton on the 31 March, 1894 in front of 23,000 fans. The other finalists were Notts County then a Second Division side that finished third that year and were obviously regarded as the underdogs for the Final.

Bolton's progress to the Final: First round; Small Heath 3–4 Bolton. Second round Newcastle United 1–2 Bolton. Third round Bolton 3–0 Liverpool. Semi-Final at Fallowfield, Manchester, Bolton 2–1 Sheffield Wed. (Goals. R1 Cassidy 2, Wilson 2. R2 Hughes, Turner. R3 Cassidy, Dickenson 2. S.F. Bentley 2.) Bolton team 1894 Cup Final: *1. J.W. Sutcliffe 2. John Sommerville 3. Di Jones 4. Alex Paton 5. Archie Hughes 6. Harry Gardiner 7. Robert Tannahill 8. Jim Wilson 9. Joseph Cassidy 10. Handel Bentley 11. Joe Dickenson.*

Shown are the Manchester, Lancashire and replica FA Cup. The original FA Cup was stolen in September, 1895 in Birmingham when it was on display in a shop window. Aston Villa the holders, then replaced it. Years later a forger admitted he had melted it down for coins and sold them on.

The game was convincingly won by Notts County 4–1, Bolton's consolation goal scored by Cassidy. Reports state that Bolton performed poorly and had fielded a number of players that were carrying substantial injuries, gambling on them being fit on the day and County being inferior opponents, which did not pay off. They seriously underestimated the desire of the County side. Strangely there does not appear to be any official programmes or advertisements of the Final for viewing. However there is a plan of the Goodison Park ground for the day with the potential teams named thereon, which is not accurate. Bolton's proposed team are named on the left of the diagram. This was the last FA Cup Final to be held at Goodison Park.

Note: Incidentally pictured with the Notts County 1894 Final team is the original FA Cup, stolen the following year.

1894 FA Cup Final players:

John William 'Willie' Sutcliffe. Born 1868 and died 1947. From Shibden, Halifax. His initial code was Rugby Union and played for Bradford and Heckmondwike. He also won an England cap against New Zealand. He switched to football and joined Bolton in 1889, though not initially as a 'keeper. He made his debut in a 7–0 win against West Brom in 1889 at Pikes Lane. He played 364 games for the club and left in 1902 after disagreements over wages. He was the first Bolton player to be sent off, in a game against Sheffield Wednesday in 1902. Bolton won the Manchester Cup 1894–95 during his time at the club and he was a runner up in the Lancashire Cup in 1899. He then played for Millwall, Manchester United and Plymouth Argyle. He finished up as coach with Southend United then abroad in 1914 at

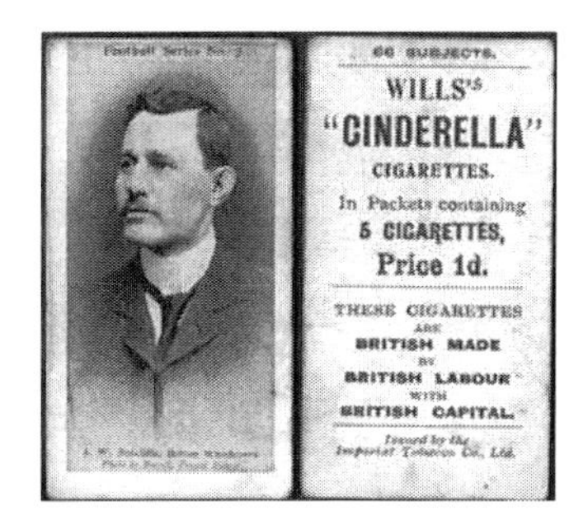

Arnhem, Holland. After the First World War he was coach at Bradford City. At Plymouth he played 214 games and was widely respected there, the Argyle handbook states, 'he was a marvel for his years'.

He represented England on five occasions, the first in 1893 against Wales in a 6–0 win, with one further unofficial game cap. He was never on the losing side. He also represented the league on three occasions. He is pictured for England and at Bolton.

John Sommerville was born in Ayr and died in 1917. He joined Bolton in 1890 from Ayr Parkhouse, later Ayr United and as a full-back formed part of the starting line-up that always began with Sutcliffe, Di Jones and himself, they were said to be that good together. His nickname was 'Johnny Surefoot'. He made his debut in a 4–0 win against Celtic. As well

He is seen here extreme right in team picture as club secretary in 1906. The team are pictured with the Manchester Cup.

as his Cup Final appearance he won a Lancashire Cup medal in 1890–91 and the Manchester Cup in 1894–95. He was also part of the promotion team back to the First Division in 1899. He was given a testimonial against Liverpool at Burnden Park on 11 October, 1897, which Bolton won 4–2. He also took part in an Anglo Scots trial match in the same year, but was not selected for the final eleven.

He was appointed secretary in 1898 and continued to play for the club until 1901. He then became the manager from 1908–10, when he was then relieved of the post but kept on as secretary until the end of the year. During his time as manager Bolton won the Manchester Cup in 1908–09. After 1910 a number of reports state he became a linesman for the Football League, he is also believed to have coached abroad in Holland.

David 'Di' Jones. Born 1867 in Trefonen, Wales and died 1902. He began his career playing at Oswestry then at Chirk winning the Welsh Cup. He signed for Bolton in 1888 as a full–back, a year in which he won his first cap for Wales. He was extremely popular and was captain by 1890 when they won the Lancashire Cup, known for his ferocious tackling, being able to play equally well with both feet. He played 255 games for the club and scored eight goals, including one in the stated Lancashire Cup Final 1890–01. He did however have the dubious honour of missing the first ever penalty kick awarded, in a match against Everton in 1892. He was also with the club when they won the Manchester Cup.

In 1898 he went to Manchester City and helped them win promotion, playing

Jones front right for Wales 1895 before a 1-1 draw against England.

in the same side as the famous Billy Meredith. He played for Wales on 14 occasions. In a practice match on 17 August, 1902 he cut his knee on glass and contracted tetanus. The infection took his life eleven days later. He was fondly remembered by both clubs and his funeral was attended by large numbers in both towns.

Alex Paton. Born in Glasgow. He began his career with Vale of Leven and appeared on the losing side in the Scottish Cup Final in 1890 against Queens Park, who won the replay 2–1, after a 1–1 draw. He chose Bolton in the same year transferring from Leven when they were still a top side; they had already captured the Scottish Cup three times and appeared in the Final on a further three occasions. He was a half-back and played 241 games for Bolton scoring 15 goals. He was injured for the 1894 Final, but played in any case, which in hindsight was probably not a good idea as he had no influence on the game at all. He won the Lancashire and Manchester Cup with Bolton. He left in 1898–89 after settling a pay dispute and playing a further six games. He seems to have disappeared off the footballing map after that and he is not listed at any other clubs on records.

Archie Hughes. Born 1870 in Neilston, Renfrewshire. He played for Barrhead and Arthurlie before going to Middlesbrough in 1892. Bolton signed him in 1893–94 season and he played 20 games scoring three goals, playing as a half-back or inside-forward. He scored one goal in the cup rounds.

In the Final he was injured after five minutes and spent the rest of the game as a virtual spectator. In 1894 he transferred to Leicester Fosse, later City. He was disciplined by them on two occasions for training abuse then sold in 1895 to Glossop, who in turn sold him to Chatham. He was reported to be back in Scotland in 1905, working as a bleacher, which was also his father's occupation.

Henry 'Harry' Gardiner. Born 1868 in Kilmarnock and died 1922. He was a centre-half and came to Bolton from Renton in 1890 until 1894, playing 84 games and scoring five goals for the club. Renton another top Scottish side, they had won the Scottish Cup in 1885 and 1888. He represented the English League against the Scottish League in 1892 at Pikes Lane, the game ending in a 2–2 draw. He gained a Lancashire Cup, runners up medal in 1892–93. After 1894 he then played a short time for Glasgow Rangers. He was reported as living in Hamilton at the time of his death. Here is the 1893–94 team again with Gardiner middle row first left.

Robert Tannahill. Born 1872 in Kilmarnock. He joined Bolton in 1892 until 1896–97. He playing 80 games and scored 11 goals. He was an outside-right by description. He played for a number of other clubs as well namely Tottenham, Millwall, Chesterfield, Fulham and Grays United. He played for Bolton during the cup season and when they won the Manchester Cup 1894–95. He is seen in the Tottenham photo sitting extreme left middle row. (Bolton photo 1893: front left).

Jim Wilson. Born in Scotland and played for Ayr Parkhouse where he played generally on the right wing. He came to Bolton in 1892–94 playing 41 games and scoring 10 goals, two on route to the Final. He then transferred to Millwall and is seen in their team photo 1894 below. (Front second left).

Joseph 'Jim' Cassidy. Born 1869 in Dalry, Scotland. Played for Glasgow Hibernians then came to Bolton in 1889 until 1897–98, making his debut against Everton. He could play in any of the forward roles. He played 219 games and scored 101 goals. He scored five goals in the clubs record 13–0 thrashing of Sheffield United in the FA Cup in 1890 and scored the clubs first penalty, he was top scorer for five seasons. 'A player of great dash and brilliance', it was reported, specifically when they headed the league table at the time in 1891. A long time Bolton supporter was reported to have said, 'I remember seeing Cassidy break the side post with a mighty shot. I saw it fall slowly to the ground'. The crowd used to shout 'shoot Cassidy' for a long time after that. During his time at Bolton he had brief loan spells with Carfin Shamrock and Celtic. He only played the one game for Celtic, but apparently almost doubled the attendance. He scored five goals in Bolton's cup campaign of 1894, including the consolation goal in the Final. He won the Lancashire Cup once and two runners up medals with Bolton in the same competition, also winning the Manchester Cup in 1894–95. After leaving Bolton he had spells with Newton Heath, Manchester City and Middlesbrough. His FA Cup medal sold at a Bonhams auction for £3,000.

Millwall 1894

Joe Dickenson played for Bolton from 1892–94, mainly as an outside-left. He was from Chatham, Kent. He played 47 games and scored 13 goals, including two in the cup campaign. He also gained a runner up medal in the Lancashire Cup 1892–93. In 1894 he transferred to New Brompton where he scored a hat-trick on his debut. He then played for his hometown club, Chatham and Grays United.

Handel Bentley born, circa 1871 was a local lad who represented Halliwell and then the YMCA before signing for Bolton in 1891 as a left sided forward. He showed great promise and qualified for an international trial in 1893. He played 50 games for the club and scored 19 goals, with two in the semi-final in Cup Final year of 1894 against Sheffield Wednesday. He is registered with the club till 1895 when he vanishes from the football scene.

These were the eleven players from the 1894 Final, though another player worthy of note in this campaign was James Albert Turner. Born 1867

in Blackbull, Goldenhill, Staffordshire, he died in 1904 in Prestwich, Lancashire aged 37. He came to Bolton Wanderers in 1888 and had been brought up in the Radcliffe area. He played 108 games for the club and scored 12 goals, with one in the cup run. He was a regular in the team at this time, but missed the Cup Final through injury, Gardiner replacing him. His usual position was as a half-back.

He won the Lancashire Cup and was twice runner up. He then played for Stoke and Derby County, again playing on the losing side in the FA Cup Final for Derby in 1898, when they lost to arch rivals Nottingham Forest 3–1, pictured middle right in the Derby side. He was capped by England whilst he was at Bolton and gained three caps in total, never playing on the losing side. He was a county level cricketer and played for Staffordshire. He retired in 1899, but only lived for a further five years.

4. 1894–95. Manchester Cup, winners for the first time. After a 0–0 draw at the Newton Heath ground in March, the reply was at Hyde Road on 8 April, 1895. The opponents were Bury and the result was a 3–2 win. Bury another quality team during this era who later won two FA Cups in 1900 and 1903. The Lancashire teams were now regarded as being the strongest group in the country.

Line-up for the replay was; Sutcliffe, Sommerville, Jones, Paton, Millar, Freebairn, Henderson, McGeachan, Andrews, Tannahill and Cassidy. (Scorers; Henderson, Tannahill, McGeachan).

Bury FC 1894–95.

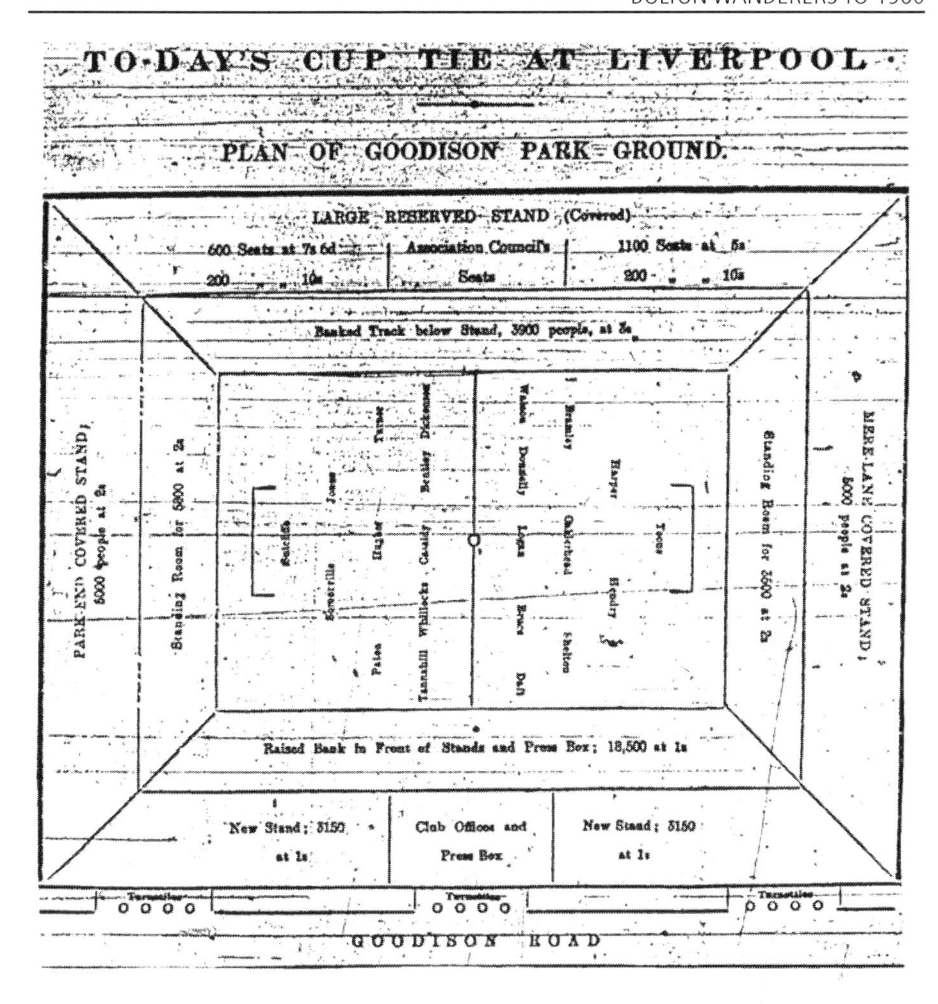

The following season 1895–96 Bolton began life at Burnden Park and reached the semi-final of the FA Cup losing 3–1 to Sheffield Wednesday at the Town Ground, Nottingham in a replay. Initial game was 1–1 at Goodison Park. Wednesday went on to win the trophy. Bolton beat Crewe, Blackpool and Bury prior to the semi-final. They also finished fourth in the First Division.

1898–99: Runners up in Lancashire Cup to Bury

3–1 at Burnden Park, though the sting in the tail was being relegated to Division Two. They bounced straight back up the following season.

5. 1903–94. FA Cup runners up. Again back in the Second Division, Bolton finished seventh and reached the semi-finals of the Manchester Cup. There progression to the Cup Final was: First round. Bolton 3–2 Reading, in a reply after a 1–1 draw at Reading. Second round. Bolton 4–2 Southampton. Third round. Sheffield United 0–2 Bolton. Semi-final. Bolton 1–0 Derby County. Played at Molineux before 20,187 fans.

In the Final they met a very strong Manchester City team that had finished runners up in the First Division. The match was at Crystal Palace in front of a 61,374 crowd on 23 April, 1904 and play was intense with Bolton holding their own throughout. The dubious only goal by Billy Meredeth was the decider with City

Scorers First round; Marsh. Replay. Freebairn,
Marsh, Yenson.
Round 2; Marsh 2, White 2.
Round 3; Marsh, Yenson.
Semi-final; Taylor.

coming out on top. Pictures of the two squads are seen. Di Davies who played in the Final is seen inset. He is not in the squad picture.

The team on the day was; 1. Dai Davies 2. Walter Brown 3. Bob Struthers 4. Robert Clifford 5. Sam Greenhalgh 6. Archie Freebairn 7. David Stokes 8. Sam Marsh 9. William Yenson 10. Wattie White 11. Robert Taylor.

THE ONLY AUTHORISED PROGRAMME.

TOPPING & SPINDLER, FLUSHING, HOLLAND.
The Oldest Established & Most Extensive Firm of Turf Commission Agents IN THE WORLD.
GREAT METROPOLITAN, CITY AND SUBURBAN, DERBY, CHESTER CUP, JUBILEE, etc.
All Letters to be addressed: TOPPING & SPINDLER, Flushing, Holland.

CRYSTAL PALACE.

OFFICIAL PROGRAMME.

English Cup Tie

MANCHESTER CITY v. BOLTON WANDERERS.

TEAMS.

MANCHESTER CITY.	BOLTON WANDERERS.
J. Hillman.	R. Taylor.
J. M'Mahon.	W. White.
Herbert Burgess.	W. Yenson.
Sam Frost.	S. Marsh.
T. Hynds.	D. Stokes.
S. B. Ashworth.	A. Freebairn.
W. Meredith.	S. Greenhalgh.
Geo. Livingstone.	Clifford.
W. Gillespie.	R. Struthers.
A. Turnbull.	W. Brown.
F. Booth.	D. Davies.

Frequent service of Trains after Match to all Parts

CRAMER PIANOS From 25 GUINEAS.

1904 Final team:

The team that played in the FA Cup Final of 1904 was part of a squad that at that time were pushing for promotion out of the Second Division, but their attentions were distracted with the run to the Cup Final. Promotion was achieved the following season 1904–05, finishing second behind Liverpool.

Players:

David 'Dai' Davies. Born 1880 and died 1944. He was from Llanelli, Wales and he initially played Rugby Union for them in 1899, but switched codes

Crystal Palace

to Rugby League in 1900 moving to Swinton, helping them to the Challenge Cup in that year scoring a try against Salford. He was signed by Bolton as goalkeeper in 1902 and stayed with them until the 1909–10. He played 137 games for the club and was capped by Wales in 1904 gaining three caps in total. After playing in the 1904 FA Cup Final he became the only player to have appeared in a Final for both codes. He broke his collarbone in 1905 and it was said that he was not quite the same player afterwards. Though after leaving the club he returned to Swinton and continued his rugby career with them until 1913, so he was obviously still capable of performing at a high physical level. Bolton won two Manchester Cups during his time at the club, in 1905–06 and 1908–09.

He retired from rugby and served with his brother also a rugby player, in the Second Salford Battalion and the Lancashire Fusiliers during the First World War. He spent some time in a French hospital with an illness not related to the fighting. After the war he was a trainer at Swinton rugby club. He lived in the area until his death.

Walter George Brown. Born in Cheadle, Manchester in 1880 and died in 1950. He was signed by Bolton in 1899, from Heywood Boys. He played for the club till 1904 with 114 appearances and could play in either full-back position. As a result of the 1904 Final he was described in the press as 'a player of stylish qualities', but was subsequently transferred to Aston Villa where he suffered a serious knee injury which affected his career. He was then transferred to Plymouth Argyle after he recovered in 1906–07. He only played one season there and then ended his career with Crystal Palace.

Robert 'Bob' Struthers. Born 1879 and died 1959. He was from Liverpool and was born near to Goodison Park. He played football locally and was then at Everton in 1897. He then turned up at Portsmouth after playing for Gravesend United. He was a full-back and played for Bolton between 1901

and 1906–07, playing 141 games before moving on to Bradford Park Avenue. He was with Bolton when they won the Manchester Cup in 1905–06. In the Cup Final year he was top of the appearance charts for the club. During the First World War he reached the rank of Major.

Struthers is seen above in the named squad photo at Burnden Park in 1903-4.

Struthers seen back row second from right

Robert 'Bob' Clifford. Born 1883 in Rankinston, Ayrshire. He came to Bolton in 1903 from Trabbock, Scotland and stayed till season 1908–09, when he moved on to Everton with Wattie White. He was there till 1911 before finishing his career at Fulham. He made 167 appearances for Bolton and scored six goals. He was with Bolton during the time they won the Manchester Cup in 1905–06 and 1908–09 as well as appearing in the FA Cup Final.

Samuel 'Sam' Greenhalgh. Born 1882 and died 1955. He was from Eagley, Bolton and played for them, Birtenshaw Wesleyans and Turton before joining Bolton in 1902 as a centre-half. He spent one year at Aston Villa in 1905, but returned to Bolton the following season. He played

278 games and scored 20 goals. He moved to Chorley in 1913–14 and played for them till 1919, he then retired to run the Cheetham Arms in Dunscar, Bolton. During his time at Bolton they won the Manchester Cup in 1905–06 and 1908–09. He represented the Football League in 1905 against the Scottish League. He won the Second Division championship with Bolton in 1909 and captained the club during this period.

Archie Freebairn. Born 1873 and died 1917. He was from Glasgow and played for Wheatburn and Partick Thistle as a half-back. His brothers Willie and David were also at the club, though Willie died in 1900 after being kicked in the chest during a game and succumbed to complications while he was being operated on. Archie joined Bolton in 1894 and played 315 games scoring 10 goals, with one on the way to the Cup Final. He was a Lancashire Cup runner up in 1898–09 and became captain in 1899 after Di Davies left and it was reported that he spread his enthusiasm all over the pitch. He was with Bolton till 1906–07 and after recovering from injury played in the FA Cup Final. He was part of the squad that secured the Manchester Cup twice. He holds the record for most consecutive appearances for Bolton as an outfield player at 135. He spent the latter part of his career at Bolton in the reserves due to injuries. His death was reported in the Liverpool Echo in 1917.

David 'Spider' Stokes was born 2 February, 1878 in Ketley, Staffordshire. He resided in the area playing his football locally before signing for Kingswinford Albion then Bolton in 1901–02 after a league enquiry which ended in Bolton receiving a ten guinea fine, though they still managed to get him despite Aston Villa's protests, stating they had reputedly put him on their books. He was an outside right and made his debut in 1902. He made

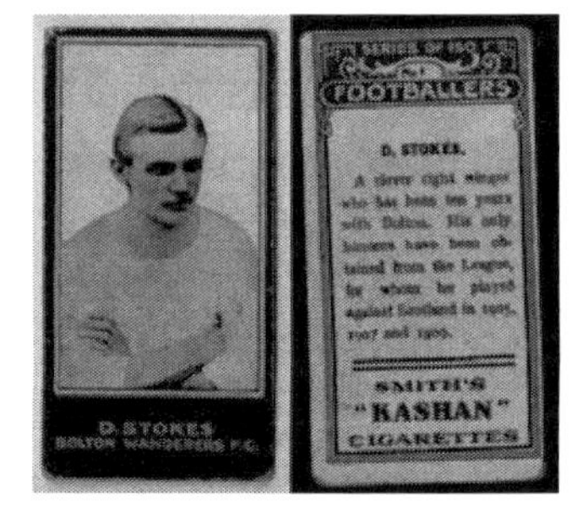

420 appearances and scored 46 goals. As well as appearing in the Cup Final he helped secure two Manchester and one Lancashire Cup win. He also helped Bolton to the Second Division title in 1909 and represented the Football League on four occasions, three against Scotland and once against the Irish. He was described as the best winger never to be selected for international honours.

During the war he was a munitions worker, but still played for Bolton till 1919 aged 39. In 1920 he returned to play for Brierley Hill and was signed for one season by Wolves in 1920–21 aged 40, playing in the Second Division. He then retired in the Kingswinford area and was caretaker of the local Conservative Club. He died in 1969 aged 91 years at his home.

He was the Uncle of Ray Westwood and described as having similar attributes. A football report of the time read, 'Stokes could beat an opponent neatly and cleverly, it took a fast man to keep pace with him. Whilst in ball control, dribbling, centring power and shooting, he possessed every attribute of a great forward.'

Samuel Marsh. Born 1879 in Westhoughton and played locally for Daisy Hill, Hindley and Atherton. He came to Bolton in 1902 and played till 1911–12, he then went to Bury where he finished his football career. He played 201 games for Bolton and scored 81 goals. He made his debut in 1902 and finished the club top scorer, but they were relegated. In the Cup Final year he was the clubs top scorer in the competition with five goals. He formed a fearsome partnership with Albert Shepherd and Wattie White and the year after the Final when Bolton were promoted back to the First Division they scored 65 goals between them. During his time at Bolton, Marsh played in the 1904 Final and won the Manchester Cup on two occasions. In 1909 he captained the 'Reserves' to victory in this competition beating first team opposition along the way in the shape of Manchester City and Stockport

County, the Bolton side containing a young 'Joe Smith'. On retirement Marsh ran the Ainsworth Arms in Bolton with his wife. He then goes off the radar, but appears briefly in 1935 outside Leeds United ground, Elland Road for the FA Cup semi-final against West Brom. Bolton President Sir William Edge was giving away three tickets to unemployed men, due to the depressive times that had gripped the country. A reporter for the *Evening News* spotted a dishevelled Sam Marsh, who was part of the group outside the ground. He had sadly lost his job and was struggling to make ends meet. He is not reported on or seen again thereafter and a tragic end to a very under rated player who like many others vanished into obscurity.

Philip Owen William '(Billy)' Yenson. Born in Bagpuize, Oxfordshire in 1880 and died in 1944, though there are other reports that say he was born in 1883 and was of Swedish extraction. He was known at each club as Billy or William. He initially played for West Ham before signing for Bolton in 1903 as a centre-forward, though he did later switch to half-back. He played 34 games and scored 10 goals with two in the Cup competition in 1904. He then transferred to QPR. He also played for West Ham again and then Croydon, Crystal Palace and Brentford. His final club was Margate and he retired around 1920 to run a tobacconist shop in Croydon. Both his brothers played to a high standard and his son, Kenny played for Bromley in the successful 1949 amateur FA Cup Final side against Romford, the winning score was 1–0.

Walter 'Wattie' White. Born 1882 in Hurlford, Scotland and died 1950. He played for a number of local sides and then Kilmarnock, before signing for Bolton in 1902 as an inside-forward. He played 217 games and scored 93 goals. He scored two goals in the Cup Final year and the following year scored 24 goals in 33 games. The Manchester Cup was

secured in 1905–06. He gained two Scotland caps, the first in 1907 against England. In season 1908–09 he was sold to Everton with Bob Clifford after Bolton were relegated in 1907–08. He transferred to Fulham in 1910 and played the rest of his career for them retiring in 1923 aged 40 becoming the oldest player to appear for the club, though his career with them was interrupted by the First World War. He was given a benefit game in 1926 against QPR.

He lived in Fulham till his death and was described as a diminutive skilful player with excellent ball control, who could play inside-forward, half-back or in defence.

Robert 'Bob' Taylor. Born 1876 in Daubhill, Bolton and died 1919. Played locally and was then spotted by Everton, Bolton signing him from them in 1901. He played 114 games scoring 19 goals including the only goal of the 1904 semi-final. He could play as a winger, half-back or centre-half. He was part of the squad winning the Manchester Cup in 1905–06 and Bolton is his last recorded club in 1907.

J. Boyd D. Stokes S. Marsh R. Struthers H. Baverstock R. Taylor S. Greenhalgh W. White M. McEwan D. Davies A. Shepherd

BOLTON WANDERERS F.C.

Photo: Howard Barrett, Southwell, Nottingham

It has been mistakenly reported that Archie Taylor, who signed for Bolton from Dundee in 1904 played in the Final. He in fact only played three games for the club before moving on to Bristol Rovers. He did however win the FA Cup with Barnsley in 1912 and is honoured in their club profile history.

6. 1904–05 Bolton won promotion back to the First Division and created a record of 11 consecutive wins, followed in 1905–06 with a Manchester Cup Final win. The final was played on 30 March, 1906 at Clayton against another good class Bury side. Bolton won the game 3–0.

Team on the day: Davies, Baverstock, Struthers, Gaskell, Freebairn, Boyd, Stokes, Taylor, Shepherd, White, McEwan. Goals: Boyd, White (pen), McEwan.

7. 1908–09 Manchester Cup winners. Final played on 29 April, 1909 at Hyde Road against Stockport County. Bolton won 3–0. Bolton also won the Second Division Championship in this season. Billy Hughes, top scorer that season with 15 goals, he had been signed in the same season. (He is in the 1910 team photo, (3rd row, 5th from left.)

1910 Team

Stockport County

12 Lancashire wins

8. 1911–12 Lancashire Cup winners. It had been twenty years since last capturing this sought after trophy. The club did well in the First Division in this season, finishing fourth. On route to the Final they beat Nelson 4–2, Barrow 1–0 and Man United 2–1. The Final was contested against Burnley on the 13 December, 1911 at Burnden Park in front of a crowd of 11,000. Bolton won the game with ease 4–1. The scorers were Smith, Bentley 2 and Barber.

The team line up was; 1. Newton 2. Baverstock 3. Feebury 4. Barber 5. Fay 6. Whiteside 7. Stokes 8. Hilton 9. Bentley 10. Smith 11. Vizard. (The young man front centre in the 1910 photo is Joe Smith who went on to be one of Bolton's greatest legends and prolific goal scorer setting many records and becoming team captain. Future 1920s favourites, Ted Vizard and Bill Jennings are also in the 1910 team photo.)

Bolton seemed to spend the mid 1900s yo-yoing between Division One and Two despite Cup successes. After 1911 they remained in the top flight till 1933.

1914–15: They reached the FA Cup semi-final losing to Sheffield United 2–1 at Ewood Park before 22,404 fans. The Bolton scorer was Joe Smith pictured in the souvenir. They had previously dispatched Notts County, Millwall, Burnley and Hull City.

Left is Mr Charles Foweraker, manager from 1919. He served the club until 1944 and is the clubs most successful manager.

Here is the squad in 1913–14, war was now a frightening reality.

During the first war the club used a number of guest players and notably the four listed here played key roles in games during this difficult period and are mentioned due to their significant goal contributions for Bolton.

Robert Geddes. He was born in Hurst, Manchester and was a centre-forward. He is listed playing for Bolton between 1916–18 and scored 20 goals. His other known clubs were Stalybridge and Hurst, who eventually renamed as Ashton United.

Alf Winterburn. He was from Manchester and is listed with one league game for the club in 1919–20. War League: 1916–18 with 22 goals. He was top scorer in season 1917–18 with 14 goals. He was a winger or inside-forward. He later played for Crewe and Hurst.

James 'Jimmy' Heathcote was born on 17 November, 1894 in Bolton and played for the club between 1917–19. In two seasons he scored 22 goals. A well-built forward he played for a number of clubs. He signed for Blackpool in 1919 and scored 33 goals in 89 games. Other clubs he signed for are: Notts County, Pontypridd, Lincoln City, Mansfield and Coventry City before ending his career at Accrington Stanley in 1929.

Walter Davies was born in Manchester and played between 1917–19 for Bolton. He had initially played for Hurst as an inside-forward. He scored 16 goals in the two listed seasons. He was also on Manchester United books as an amateur. He then played for Crewe scoring eight goals in 34 games, before finishing his career with Nantwich and Whitchurch.

TRIBUTES TO THE FALLEN 1914–18 CONFLICT

Research shows that a number of Bolton players participated in action during the First World War. Records also show that a number of players who had association with Bolton lost their lives: the ones who fell are listed here in tribute to their memory.

1. Lieutenant James Arthur Greenhalgh was born in 1889 in Daubhill, Bolton. His death was reported on 22/10/1914 near Voilaines, France in the Manchester Evening News. It is stated he was a good amateur player who assisted the Wanderers when required and also played for Manchester University from where he had graduated. He had been commissioned to the Cheshire Regiment in August, 1914. He then took command of his unit on the 19/10/1914, after his superior officer had been wounded. Captain Lewis later wrote to the parents of James after his death expressing his gratitude for the bravery of his actions. He is remembered at the Touret Memorial, France and at the Manchester University and Bolton Church Memorials.

2. Harold Greenhalgh (no relative) from Egerton was killed in France on the 27th June, 1916 and was a member of the Royal Field Artillery. He is listed as a full back playing for Bolton during the 1915-6 season. His death was reported in the Bolton Journal and he is buried in France.

3. Herbert Lewis Bithell was born 1893 in Holywell, Wales. He is believed to have been with Bolton around 1914-5, but joined up before he had opportunity to play for the club in May, 1915. His other clubs had been Atherton and Macclesfield. He had moved to the Bolton area with his parents and siblings, he was then employed at Denmark Mill, Farnworth. He lived on Longcauseway, Farnworth with his wife Edna who he married in October, 1915. He also taught Sunday school at Farnworth Baptist Church. He was killed on the 18/3/1918 serving with the Welsh Regiment and is remembered at the Merville Communal Cemetery, Nord, France. Sadly Edna never saw him again after he returned to France in 1915 as he remained on the western front till his death.

4. William Wallace was from Blaydon in the North East of England. He played for Manchester City as an outside left from 1912–14 with 43 appearances and eight goals. He played for Bolton between 1914–15 with two recorded games and one goal. He was then signed up into the Royal Field Artillery and posted to France for the war effort. He was killed on 8 April, 1917 and his headstone is in the Lapugnoy Military Cemetery, Pas De Calais, France. He is also seen in the earlier team photograph from 1914–15 along with Percy Toone and Joe Thomas whose Bolton careers were affected by the war, they were fortunate though as they survived the conflict. Others in the photo serving were: Smith, Vizard, Seddon, Lillycrop and Glendenning.

5. Frederick G Costello was born in 1884 in Birmingham and is linked with a number of clubs namely, West Brom, Southampton, West Ham, Nelson, Merthyr Town, Salisbury City and of course Bolton Wanderers. He made the most impression with Southampton and West Ham between 1907–09 as a forward. He was on Bolton's books between 1909–10 though he did not manage to break into the first team, moving on to Nelson FC.

In 1914 he was living in Southampton and joined the Royal Warwickshire Regiment, which was one of the first regiments to see action in Northern France. He was killed on 19 December, 1914 and is remembered at Ploegstreet Memorial, Belgium.

6. Jabez Cartwright was born in 1883 in the Worcester area and began his football career for Mapperley and Grantham Town in 1912 as a right-back. He signed for Bolton not long after this for £110 so was obviously highly regarded; yet he failed to break into the first team for unknown reasons. In 1914 he signed for Merthyr Town and at the end of that season he returned to Grantham Town. He joined the war effort with the Lincolnshire Regiment and was killed in action on 4 October, 1917. He is remembered at the Tyne Cot Memorial, Belgium.

CLUB SUCCESS 1920–1939

1. 1920–01 Manchester Cup winners against Man United. The score was 2–0 at Burnden Park on 11 May, 1921. They were also runners up in the Lancashire Cup losing 2–1 to Manchester City at Old Trafford. This was a fine season for Bolton, again achieved their highest ever Division One position of third. (Burnley finished as the league winners.)

Manchester United have 15 Lancashire Cup wins

2. 1921–22. Another good league season and wins in both the Lancashire and Manchester Cups. The Lancashire Cup on a league basis, disposing of Everton and Liverpool, before beating Man City in a semi-final replay 1–0 and the great decade was now truly taking shape.

Pictured are the Bolton squad of 1922 with the very large impressive Lancashire Cup after the defeat of Bury. Roberts transferred to Manchester City after this photograph was taken.

The Lancashire final was held on 17 May, 1922 at Gigg Lane, against Bury, before a crowd of 15,912. The score in Bolton's favour 3–1 with goals from Roberts (2) and Smith (Pen).

Team; 1. Pym. 2. Haworth 3. Rowley 4. Longworth 5. Seddon 6. Buchan 7. Butler 8. Jack 9. Roberts 10. Smith 11. Vizard.

Manchester City 1920. They have six Lancashire Cup wins.

Back: Longworth, Nuttall, Haworth, Pym, Rowley, Buchan and Jones.
Front: Butler, Jack, Roberts, Seddon, J. Smith, Vizard, Jennings.

Three days later on 20 May, 1921 they secured the Manchester Cup at Old Trafford against Eccles United with a 3–1 win. It was now that Bolton Wanderers were really being talked about as one of the country's top first class outfits and courted much publicity as championship contenders.

Bury have nine Lancashire Cup wins

3. 1922–23 FA Cup winners. Perhaps the most famous publicity laden season in Bolton Wanderers history that needs no introduction to any football fan with even limited knowledge of the game. This was too well and truly put Wanderers on the world stage. The final was the first ever held at the new Wembley Stadium on 28 April, 1923, so fate played its part. The opponents being West Ham United, who were at the time a Second Division

team, but they finished second that year to be promoted into the First Division.

George Kay, back row fourth from left, the captain of the West Ham side played for Bolton between 1910–11 and later managed Liverpool, before working for Bill Shankly. He is seen at Bolton in the earlier photograph from 1910.

The scene on the day was complete chaos and over 126,047 fans were registered as in the stadium. Though unofficially it was probably a lot nearer 200,000, other reports state there were upto 300,000. Seen here is a view of the crowds, it was utter chaos.

West Ham 1923 Final Team

David Jack scores the opening goal in the Final and other match scenes from the *Sunday Pictorial* report of the game. The best that could be achieved was having the crowd lining the edge of the pitch due the volume of fans in the stadium. On the day Bolton won the game by 2–0 with the second goal being scored by John Reid Smith.

Route to Final: First round; Norwich 0–2 Bolton. J. Smith. J. R. Smith. Second round; Bolton 3–1 Leeds. Jack 2. J. Smith. Third round; Huddersfield Town 1–1 Bolton. Jack. Replay; Bolton 1–0

SUNDAY·PICTORIAL

Jack scores the first ever Wembley goal

Huddersfield Town. Jack. Fourth round; Charlton Athletic 0–1 Bolton. Jack. Semi-final at Old Trafford Bolton 1–0 Sheffield United. Jack. (Note: They beat Huddersfield Town on route to the Final, they were to win the League Championship for the next three consecutive years which showed the quality of the Bolton squad).

David Jack scored in every round except the first and was already very popular and soon to become a much sought player after the final due to its extensive publicity.

4. 1924–25 Lancashire Cup winners. The final was played at Burnden Park before 11,292 fans. The opponents were Blackpool and the result in Bolton's favour 2–1 with goals from Jack and Nuttall. On the way they beat Stockport 4–0, Southport 3–1 and Everton 4–1.

The team was; 1. Pym 2. Greenhalgh 3. Finney 4. Nuttall 5. Seddon 6. Jennings 7. Butler 8. Jack 9. Cassidy 10. Smith 11. Vizard .

In the league they again achieved a third place finish in Division One with a record 17 home wins.

5. 1925–26 FA Cup winners. The final at Wembley on 24 April, 1926 against Manchester City their nemesis from 1904 was played in front of 91,447 fans. As befitted any Cup Final now there was a lot of publicity as seen from the advertisements. Route to Final: Third round; Accrington 1–0, Jack. Fourth round; Bournemouth 2–2, J.R. Smith, Jack and 6–2 in replay, Boston, J. Smith 2, Jack, J.R. Smith 2. Fifth round: South Shields 3–0, J. Smith, Jack, J.R. Smith. Sixth round; Nottingham Forest 2–2 Butler 2, 0–0 and 1–0, J. Smith. Semi-final: Bolton beat

The above advertisement guesses at the final line up and shows Baggett and Rollo Jack, J.R Smith is omitted. The actual line up is seen in the programme from the day below.

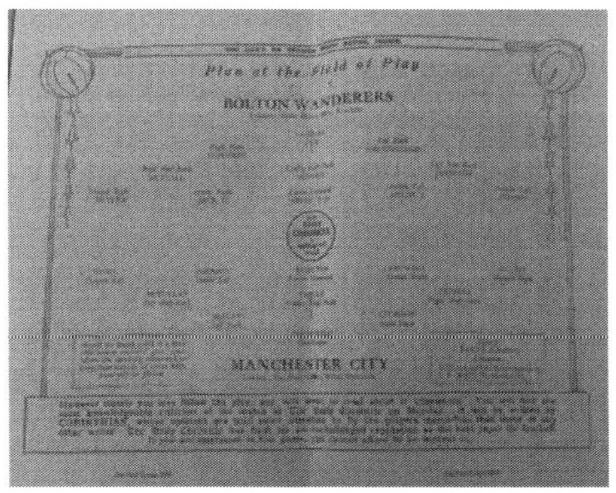

The Wanderers were now widely regarded in Europe. Above is a French postcard for the Final.

Swansea 3–0 at White Hart Lane: scorers were Baggett and Joe Smith 2, 1 pen before 25,476.

This was a keenly contested match but Bolton was the better side and a goal from David Jack sealed a second victory within three years.

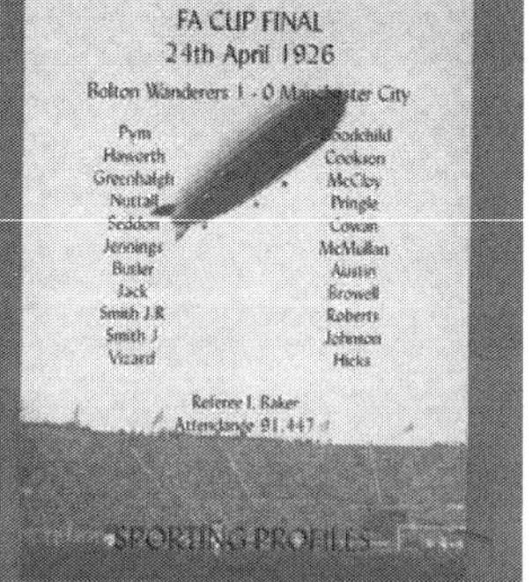

FA CUP FINAL
24th April 1926

Bolton Wanderers 1 - 0 Ma[illegible]ster City

Pym	[illegible]odchild
Haworth	Cookson
Greenhalgh	McCloy
Nuttall	Pringle
Seddon	Cowan
Jennings	McMullan
Butler	Austin
Jack	Browell
Smith J.R	Roberts
Smith J	Johnson
Vizard	Hicks

Referee I. Baker
Attendance 91,447

SPORTING PROFILES

Jack scores the winner watched by Joe and John Reid Smith.

The result from The Sporting Profile and a 1926 winner's medal

6. 1926–27 Lancashire Cup winners. They beat Everton 2–1, Burnley 3–0 and Man City 6–1 to get there.

7. The Final played at Burnden Park on 14 May, 1927 against Bury. The score 1–0 and the scorer was Joe Smith. The crowd on the day was 13,229. The team was; 1. Pym 2. Greenhalgh 3. Finney 4. Cope 5. Seddon 6. Nuttall 7. Butler 8. Jack 9. Smith 10. Gibson 11. Vizard. Below is another 1920s team photo. Joe Smith the captain, holding the ball. Another good league season as well, finishing fourth.

Bury had won the Lancashire Cup the previous season beating Accrington Stanley 5–2

8. 1928–29 FA Cup winners and third Wembley appearance of the decade. The opponents being another First Division side Portsmouth. The attendance was 92,576. Below is the programme cover for the day.

1928 team on tour in Europe

The result, 2–0 with goals from Butler and Blackmore and the third FA Cup victory of the decade was secured. Below Butler, Seddon and McClelland with the FA Cup. Ted Vizard has the match ball.

The following players played in all three FA Cup competitions and have the rare honour of three FA Cup winner medals. 1. Dick Pym, 2. Bob Haworth, 3. Harry Nuttall, 4. James Seddon, 5. Billy Butler.

Alex Finney played in the 1923 and 1929 Finals. He would most probably have played in all three

Presented with BOYS' MAGAZINE.

THE F.A. CUP FINALISTS, 1929.

BOLTON WANDERERS F.C.

Back Row—R. HAWORTH, A. FINNEY, R. H. PYM, J. SEDDON, H. NUTTALL.
Front Row—F. W. KEAN, W. BUTLER, J. McCLELLAND, H. A. BLACKMORE, G. R. GIBSON, W. COOK.

PORTSMOUTH F.C.

Back Row—R. IRVINE, J. A. MACKIE, J. GILFILLAN, J. McCOLGAN.
Front Row—F. FORWARD, J. W. SMITH, J. NICHOL, J. WEDDLE, J. McILWAINE, D. THACKERAY, D. WATSON, F. COOK.

but was injured in 1926 with cartilage problems. Jennings, J.R. Smith, J. Smith, Jack and Vizard all played in the 1923 and 1926 Finals.

1928–29 and 1930–31 Bolton won the Richardson Cup and they also secured the West Lancashire Cup in 1930–31.

The main body of the team had survived throughout the 1920s, but as the 1930s began it was to be a period of re-building. A new generation of heroes were about to break through after a stuttering start to the early period of the next decade.

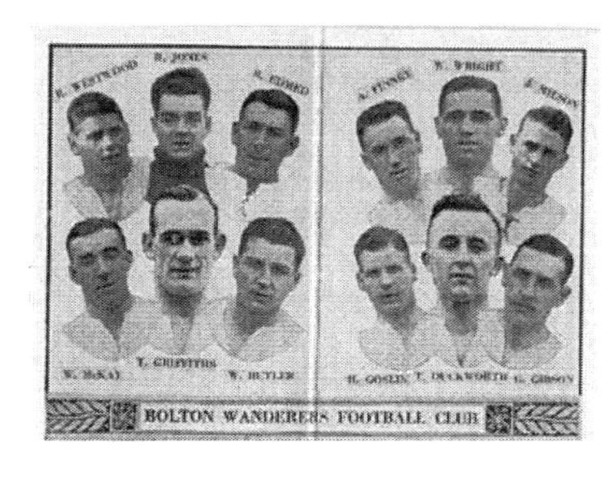

9. 1931-2 Lancashire Cup winners. Played at Maine Road on 14 May, 1932 the opponents were fellow First Division side Manchester City before a crowd of 15,386. The score in Bolton's favour 3–2 with goals from McKay, Gibson and Cook with Matt Busby in the City team. They beat Accrington Stanley 4–1, Liverpool 8–1 and Blackpool 5–1, all in replays to get to the Final.

Team: 1. Jones 2. Duckworth 3. Finney 4. McKay 5. Griffiths 6. Haworth 7. Butler 8. Gibson 9. Milsom 10. Westwood 11. Cook. Below a mid-1930s team photo:

Westwood was to be a particular favourite and without doubt would have been far greater but for the war. Jack Milsom was a prolific goal scorer and in 253 games for the club scored 153 goals. He transferred to Manchester City in 1938. Yet in season 1932–33 his goals could not stop the clubs poor form and they slid into the Second Division. They did however reach the Final of the Lancashire Cup, losing at Anfield to Liverpool 2–1.

Oldham have three Lancashire Cup wins

10. 1933–34. Lancashire Cup winners. This season they finished third missing promotion by a point, but secured the Cup. Played at Maine Road before 6,173 on 12 May, 1934, the opponents were Oldham Athletic also from Division Two. The score was 4–2 with goals from Westwood 2, Eastham

1933 Manchester City with Matt Busby second row, third from left next to 'keeper Frank Swift, whose brother played for Bolton.

and G.T. Taylor. They beat Burnley 3–0, Accrington Stanley 5–2 and Man City 3–2 to get there.

The team was: 1. R. Jones 2. Smith 3. Finney 4. Goslin 5. Atkinson 6. G.Taylor 7. G.T. Taylor 8. Eastham. 9. E. Jones 10. Westwood. 11. Cook

11. Season 1934–35 Bolton finished second behind Brentford and returned to the top flight. They struggled at first but under the leadership of captain Harry Goslin they began to gain momentum and once again become a quality outfit, reaching the semi-final of the FA Cup. They lost to West Brom in a reply at Stoke 2–0 after a mammoth campaign. Along the way they also played Tottenham Hotspur three times, eventually overcoming them at Villa Park 2–0. The Tottenham game at White Hart Lane attracted 70,347 fans with over 47,000 watching the Burnden encounter. (Sheffield Wednesday won the FA Cup that season.) By 1937 they had climbed

SHERMAN'S SEARCHLIGHT ON FAMOUS TEAMS

BOLTON WANDERERS

(Founded in 1887)

Principal Honours: F.A. Cup winners, 1922–23; 1925–26; 1928–29. Champions Div. II, 1908–09. Runners-up Div. II, 1899–1900; 1904–05; 1910–11; 1934–35.

THE club was first known as Bolton Christ Church F.C. They played on various grounds and one of their members suggested that they should call themselves the "Wanderers." This was adopted and the name has remained with them ever since.

The Wanderers joined the League upon its formation in 1888 but have never been successful in winning the Championship of the First Division.

Their memorable Cup Final of 1923, the first ever held at Wembley Stadium, will remain unforgotten, if only for the fact that the start of the game had to be delayed, owing to the huge crowd that covered the playing pitch. Bolton beat West Ham that day, and won the trophy again three years later when they beat Manchester City. Another space of three years saw them at Wembley once more—in the final of 1929—when the Wanderers defeated Portsmouth.

NAMES OF PLAYERS (Left to right looking at photograph).

Back row - Goslin, Milsom, Atkinson, Mr. R. Young (Trainer), Swift, Hurst, Grosvenor, Connor.
Sitting - - - - - - - Howe, Tennant, Carruthers, Hubbick, Taylor, G., Calder.
On ground - - - - - - - - - - - - Geldard, Westwood, Anderson.

"SHERMAN'S COMPLETE SERVICE" includes a series of photographs and biographies of the most famous Soccer Teams, and are issued weekly.

Issued by SHERMAN'S POOLS LTD., ST. MARY STREET, CARDIFF, 1938–39

Fred Swift the pictured 'keeper was as stated brother to famous Man City keeper Frank Swift.

to a respectable seventh in the First Division with Goslin leading the side.

In 1939 Goslin will always be remembered as the man who gave the rousing speech before the Sunderland game at Burnden in April, delivering the message that every person has a duty to serve the cause against the Germans, the whole team then famously signing up for the war effort. This is immortalised in the book *Wartime Wanderers* and a film was also commissioned. Unfortunately Harry Goslin, pictured was killed in action in Italy in 1943 and is buried in Cheti Province, Italy. He was greatly missed by all and will never be forgotten.

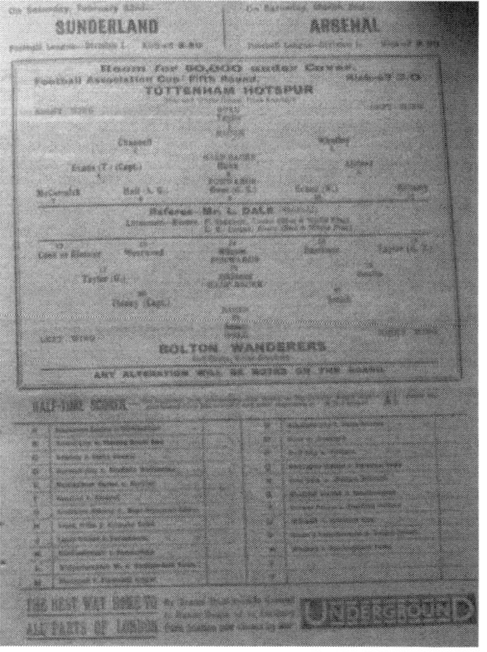

SUNDERLAND

ARSENAL

Room for 60,000 under Cover.

Football Association Cup Fifth Round.

TOTTENHAM HOTSPUR

Referee—Mr. L. DALE

BOLTON WANDERERS

ANY ALTERATION WILL BE NOTED ON THE BOARD.

HALF-TIME SCORES

UNDERGROUND

Goslin had replaced James Seddon as the leader figure of the side and club captain, playing a similar footballing role. Harry Goslin took up this mantle with great dignity.

Pictured is the programme from the away leg of the FA Cup fifth round game on 15 February, 1935, which attracted the large White Hart Lane crowd for the 1–1 draw.

12. 1937–38 Manchester Cup winners. The opponents this year were Manchester United at Old Trafford on 14 May, 1938, Bolton winning the game 2–1. Then in the Second Division, United were rebuilding after almost being liquidated in the early 1930s, but they gained promotion in this season. Hard to believe but true. During the 1930s Bolton appeared in this semi-final six times in total, which shows their commitment to it and along with the Lancashire Cup were still strongly contested competitions.

13. 1938–39 as war fast approached the Lancashire Cup was secured, or at least shared. The opponents were Preston North End who finished ninth in the First Division, just behind Wanderers. The game was at Deepdale on 10 May, 1939. The score 1–1 with Bolton's goalscorer George Hunt, signed from Arsenal in 1938. The team on the day:

1. Hanson 2. Winter 3. Hubbick 4. Goslin 5. Atkinson 6. Hurst 7. Geldard 8. Sinclair 9. Hunt 10. Westwood 11. Rothwell

Preston have six Lancashire Cup wins

WAR YEARS AND WAR CUP 1939–45

As seen above the whole Bolton Wanderers team had signed up for the war effort. Football League matches were suspended as was the FA Cup and Bolton stood at sixth in the First Division when the suspension was put in place. Players were eligible when on leave to play and the younger players were brought through to assist. There was also non-conscripted men and reserved occupations, like mining. Harry Hubbick was a miner and George Hunt served in the Police with Jack Atkinson, though Atkinson later served with the 53rd Lancashire Field Regiment as a truck driver.

The war leagues were formed and Bolton did struggle after 1940 until the latter stages of the war due in the main to the loss of so many players, unsettled sides and rebuilding of the team. They were then runners up in the 1943–44 Lancashire Cup Final to Liverpool, over two legs by 6–3. Almost 27,000 ration-restricted fans watched these two

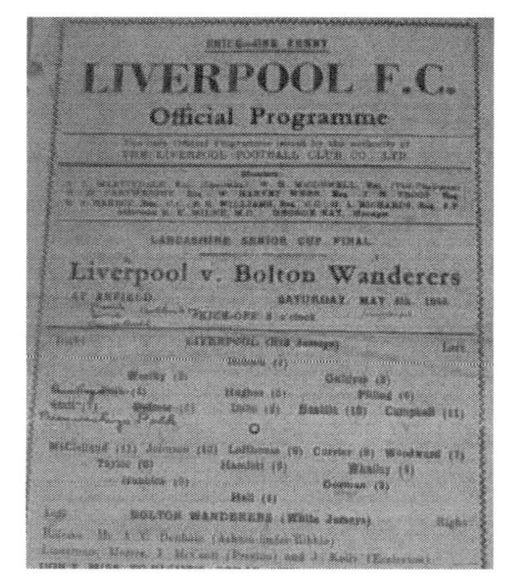

LIVERPOOL F.C.

Official Programme

LANCASHIRE SENIOR CUP FINAL

Liverpool v. Bolton Wanderers

BOLTON WANDERERS

1943-4 Lancashire Cup Final programme:

matches. The programme with team line ups for the Liverpool away game is pictured. (It was the same for both fixtures.)

Guest Players in Final for Bolton: Hall ('Keeper), Gorman (Full-Back), Whalley (Half-Back), Johnson (Inside-Forward) and McClelland (Winger).

Goals for Bolton: Lofthouse 1, Currier 1 and 1 own goal.

Bolton needed to remain in a financially stable position and until 1944 Mr Foweraker was looking after its fortunes, but his health was now poor and the club like many others was finding ways to keep going. Walter Rowley a long time Bolton player and trainer who was in the 1923 Cup Final squad was handed the reins. The club was now actively using its youth players and scouting system as well as using the loan and war guest player option, as all clubs were allowed to do this for the war league and cup games.

In 1939 a 14-year-old youth called Nathaniel Lofthouse was signed by Mr Foweraker. A fanatical Bolton supporter, he idolised the team and in particular Ray Westwood and George Hunt. His favourite was Ray Westwood and he deeply respected Hunt. He states; "I could learn more playing and training with George Hunt in one hour, than most people could learn in a day". Hunt used to train Lofthouse and one particular method which Nat described, was to have him wear a slipper on his right foot. This was to improve his shooting with the left foot. Lofthouse said Hunt never lost his temper and was always controlled. He only did it after explaining it would make me a better all-round player. Nat made his debut alongside Hunt on 12 March, 1941.

During this period there was the unofficial, as many people viewed it FA Cup, the War Cup. It was usual to play teams from within your region, due to shortages in petrol and resources. In 1942–43 it was divided into, north and south sections. The winners of each section then played off in an overall Final. All the major teams took part and it was taken very seriously indeed. It filled the void left by the cancellation of the FA Cup and undoubtedly boosted people's moral.

It began in 1939–40 and the first winners were West Ham with a 1–0 defeat of Blackburn Rovers at Wembley despite the threat of bombing raids.

1940–41 winners: Preston N.E. 2–1 in a replay at Ewood Park after a 1–1 draw at Wembley v Arsenal. Preston also won the North League section, so in effect they won the double.

1941–42 winners: Wolverhampton Wanderers against Sunderland, in the only two leg Final of the war on a 6–2 aggregate.

1942–43 winners: North section was Blackpool over two legs v Sheffield Wednesday (4–3).

South section was Arsenal one leg only. 7–1 against Charlton Athletic.

Final: Blackpool 4–2 Arsenal at Stamford Bridge.

1943–44 winners: North section was Aston Villa over two legs v Blackpool (5–4).

South section was Charlton over one leg. 3–1 against Chelsea.

Final: Charlton 1–1 Aston Villa at Stamford Bridge. (Shared –no replay).

1944–45 War Cup:

It was now the turn of Bolton. They qualified for the North Final and had disposed of Accrington Stanley 4–0, Blackpool 5–3 and Newcastle 5–4 all aggregate scores. It was Wolves in the semi-final with a 2–2 draw away, goals coming from Barrass and Butler. A 2–1 home win sealed victory with goals from Moir and Hunt. The away leg teams are displayed in the programme.

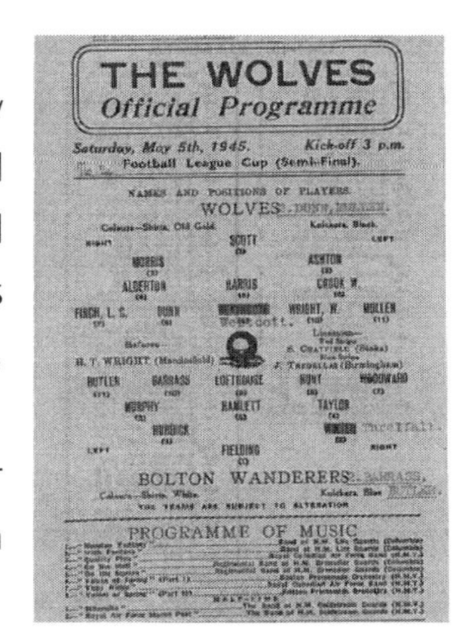

The Northern Final legs were against Manchester United, at home on 19 and away on 26 May, 1945. The results 1–0 at home with a Lofthouse goal and 2–2 away making Bolton the Northern winners. At this stage Lofthouse had scored 11 goals in the competition and was fast becoming the linchpin of the Bolton team, including the only goal of the first leg of the regional Final. In fact he had been doubtful for the second leg against United and the town was almost in mourning at the prospect of him missing the game. In the end he played, but it was Malcolm Barrass another future England player and Bolton legend who scored both the goals at Maine Road, as Old Trafford had been bomb damaged. The home leg was watched by 40,785 and the away leg by 57,395.

The National Final was held at Stamford Bridge against Chelsea who had beaten Millwall in the Southern final over one leg 2–0. The final was on 2 June, 1945 before 45,000. Chelsea scored first, but replies by Hunt then a penalty by Lol Hamlett sealed the Bolton victory for a fantastic win and achievement for a team virtually re-built from the start of the war, though it is only fair to say that a lot of teams had suffered a similar fate. This greatly lifted the spirit of the town and the team were well received back home, both after the Northern and National finals.

The only change from the North Final was Willie Moir. He had signed as an amateur in 1943 and replaced Butler, who had played the majority

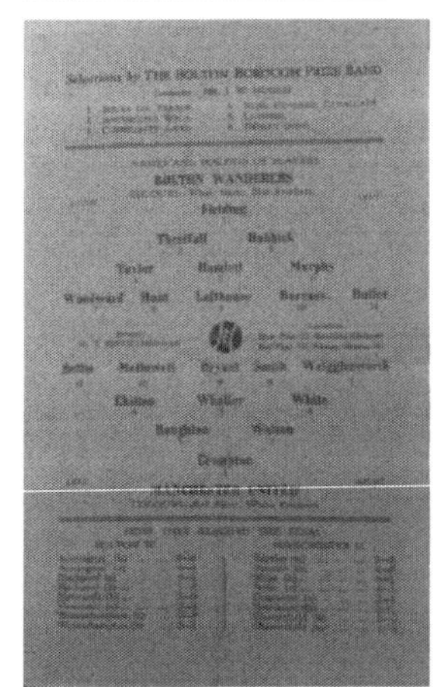

Home leg programme.

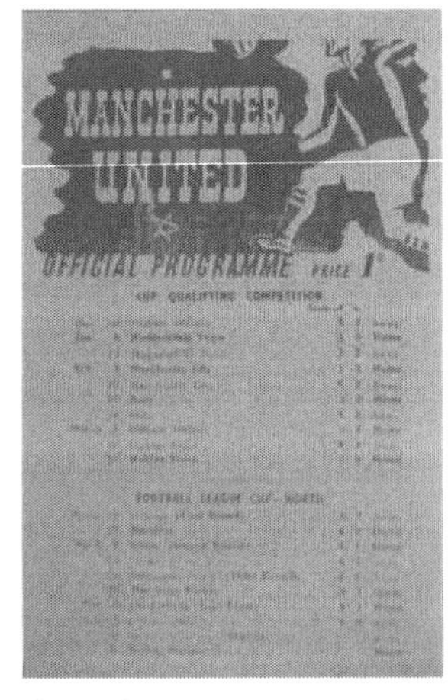

Away leg programme.

Above is the triumphant procession through Bolton after the North Final victory

OFFICIAL PROGRAMME
CHELSEA FOOTBALL & ATHLETIC CO., LTD.

2nd JUNE, 1945. Price: ONE PENNY

FOOTBALL LEAGUE
NORTH v. SOUTH CUP WINNERS

CHELSEA
(ROYAL BLUE)

Kick-Off 3 p.m.

Cfn. BLACK, I. H.

Cpl. COWAN, R. F/Sgt. HARDWICK, G.

Cfn. RUSSELL, R. HARRIS, J. (Capt.) FOSS, S. R.

S/I WARDLE, G. Pte. MACHIN, A. Sgt. ROOKE, R. GOULDEN, L. L/S. BAIN, J.

Referee—Comdr. G. CLARK (Royal Navy)

MOIR, W. BARRASS, M. W. LOFTHOUSE, N. HUNT, G. S. WOODWARD, T.

MURPHY, D. HAMLETT, T. L. TAYLOR, G.

HUBBICK, H. (Capt.) THRELFALL, J. R.

FIELDING

BOLTON WANDERERS
(WHITE)

The GRAND CLAPHAM JUNCTION

FIG LEAVES AND APPLE SAUCE

OUT OF ALL PROPORTION

of the cup games. Moir became a future Bolton legend and captained the team in the 1950s, including the 1953 Cup Final. He was capable of playing in a number of positions.

Wolves 1945–46

War Cup 1944–45 players

This Cup win has not been overly publicised or given its rightful place in football historical records, due mainly to readjustment after the war and the rehabilitation of the country. Make no mistake though it was still important to all the clubs and their supporters. It deserves recognition as a competition to equal any other and all the clubs taking part were still first class sides, watched by large enthusiastic crowds. It brought great joy to the people of this country during a turbulent period and greatly assisted in its recovery after

Manchester United 1945

Chelsea FC

the conflicts during the six years of war. Bolton ended this period with a sound structure in place, which put them in good stead for the coming years into the 1950s. The 1946 FA Cup when Bolton reached the semi-finals is also another much overlooked Cup campaign, as the country was still smothered by post war activities and events.

Squad list:

William 'Bill' John Fielding was born on 17 June, 1915 in Broadhurst, Cheshire. He died in May, 2006 in Lytham St Annes aged 90 years. He was with Cardiff City before the war, after joining them from Hurst in 1936, playing 50 games up until 1939. During the war he guested for Stockport County and then played for Bolton. He did sign for the club in 1944, but is not registered with any league games before he transferred to Manchester United in 1947 as cover for their injured 'keeper Jack Crompton. He was the main stay in goal for Wanderers during in the War Cup campaign, playing in both the regional and national finals. He is pictured above left.

Joseph Richard 'Dick' Threlfall seen left was born on 5 March, 1916 and died in 1994 aged 78 years. He was born in Ashton-under-Lyne and played locally for Moseley FC. He is registered with Bolton for 1946–47 as a full back with 11 games, playing during the war and throughout the 1944–45 and 45–46 season. In 1947 he transferred to Halifax FC and played over 30 games for them before reverting to a job at Ashton Gas Works for more job security, although Bolton had tried to sign him.

Harry Hubbick. Born 12 November, 1910 at Jarrow, Northumberland and died 18 March, 1992 in Preston aged 81 years. He was a full-back signed from Burnley in 1937 and played for the club until 1947 with 144 league and cup games. He was a miner during the war and played for Bolton and Blackpool, winning War Cups with both clubs. He later played for Port

Vale and Rochdale before taking coaching roles after qualifying as an FA coach, at Accrington, Bury, Halifax and Preston. He was at Bolton when they won the Manchester Cup in 1938 and played in the losing side in the Lancashire Cup Final in 1944. He was part of the FA Cup team that reached the semi-finals in 1945–46.

George Taylor. Born Ashton-under-Lyne in 1908 and believed to have died around 1972 in Bolton. He was awarded a testimonial in 1968 for long service; he had been at the club for over 50 years. He was coach when Bolton won the Lancashire Cup in 1948 and on the coaching staff for the FA Cup in 1958. He was a half-back and played 244 league and cup games scoring three goals, after originally joining as an amateur in 1926. He won a Lancashire Cup winners medal in 1933–34 and a runner up medal in 1943–44. He was also with Bolton when they won the Manchester Cup in 1937–38. He was an integral part of the team that won the War Cup and played in the War League, thus extending his career.

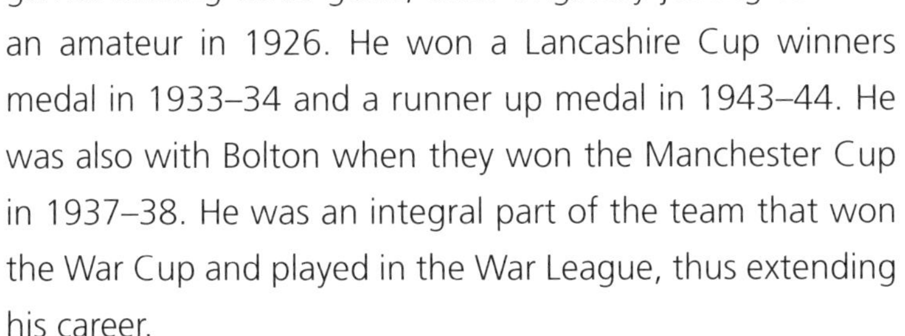

Tom 'Lol' Hamlett was born 24 January, 1917 in Stoke-on-Trent and died 22 June, 1986 aged 69 years. He initially joined Bolton from Congleton prior to the Second World War, but this seriously affected his career and he was part of the Africa Campaign. He then guested for Stoke and Manchester United during the war before again playing for Bolton from 1943–44. He is officially listed with the club from 1946–49 playing 85 games scoring nine goals. He was a central-defender and full-back. He was an integral part of the team in the War Cup and scored the winning goal in the national final against Chelsea from a penalty. It was a nervous incident, as a Chelsea fan had ran onto the pitch and stolen the ball. After

much confusion the ball was retrieved and he duly dispatched the ball into the Chelsea net.

He was part of the Bolton side that finished runners up to Liverpool in the Lancashire Cup in 1943–44 and reached the FA Cup semi- inal in 1945–46. He transferred to Port Vale in 1949 and played 109 games for them before managing Congleton in 1952. He was awarded a testimonial by Port Vale in 1976 against a Don Revie eleven. He was a religious man and never swore. He was known for use of the phrase 'fizzing' in preference to other well-used phrases! He is pictured bottom right on the previous page as a youthful Bolton player.

Daniel 'Danny' Murphy was born 10 May, 1922. Date of death 2001. He was from Burtonwood and joined Bolton in 1946 playing in the FA Cup run to the semi-final. He signed during the war and his position was a wing-half. He has 76 other registered games scoring one goal. He was a regular during the War Cup success scoring one goal. After leaving Bolton in 1951 he played for Crewe and Rochdale playing over 100 games for both clubs.

Tom Woodward was born 8 December, 1917 in Westhoughton and died 18 November, 1994. Pictured below right, he was a local lad playing for White Horse Temperance as a winger or midfielder, before signing for Bolton in 1935 making his debut in 1936 against Stoke City. He was likened to Matthews and Finney in the way he played and was similar in movement, being very strong physically. His career was interrupted like many others by the war and he became a Physical Training Instructor, whilst continuing to play for the club. He played 169 recorded games for Bolton with 19 goals. He scored two goals in the War Cup games of 1944–45. He played in the losing Lancashire Cup Final in 1943–44 against Liverpool and then in 1947–48 gained a winners medal against Southport. He was with Bolton when they won the Manchester and

Lancashire Cup in 1938 and 1939 and was part of the FA Cup campaign in 1946. He left Bolton in 1949–50 for Middlesbrough before finished his career at Wigan Athletic.

He was honoured for his services to Westhoughton and football in 2002. His portrait hangs in the Westhoughton library with another favourite Francis Lee. Above his widow Alice at the unveiling with Bolton legend Roy Hartle and the portrait artist Ray White.

George Samuel Hunt. Born 22 February, 1910 near Rotherham, Yorkshire and died on the 19 September, 1996 after suffering from Alzheimer's in his last years. He had trials locally and his grandfather had played for Barnsley, but Chesterfield signed him in 1929 where he immediately attracted much interest, inheriting the nickname 'The Chesterfield tough'. Tottenham signed him in 1930 where he played 185 games and scored 125 goals. He moved to Arsenal in 1937 and won a First Division League winner's medal with them in the one season he was there, but only scored three goals. He was transferred to Bolton in 1938 and by this time he had won three England caps with one goal.

He scored 21 goals in 18 games in the 1938–39 season as Bolton finished eighth, but war was then declared. He served in the Reserve Police Force during the conflict and continued to play for Bolton when duties permitted. He played 51 recorded games and scored 26 goals, though the War League and Cup games are not included here. He actually scored 98 goals in total before transferring to Sheffield Wednesday in 1946 after reaching the FA Cup semi-final with Bolton, scoring two goals in

that campaign. He was a great influence on the career of a young Nat Lofthouse who he showed tremendous guidance to. He scored three goals in the War Cup campaign success and won the Lancashire Cup with Bolton in 1939 in a shared final after a 1–1 draw with Preston, scoring Bolton's goal. After retiring he returned to Bolton in a training capacity until 1968 and was on the staff when they won the FA Cup in 1958. On leaving the game he ran a carwash business in the Bolton area.

Lofthouse is detailed in the section of the book dedicated to him. Note that through In the War Cup campaign he netted 11 goals and was the top scorer. In fact between 1940–41 and 1946 before the League and Cup resumed in full he scored 100 goals. He is pictured above in a 1940s training photograph.

Malcolm Williamson Barrass. Born 15 December, 1924 in Blackpool and died on the 4 August, 2013 in Manchester. He signed for Bolton in 1944; his father had played for Sheffield Wednesday and Manchester City. Malcolm played 357 recorded games and scored 27 goals. He was an attacking midfielder and defender becoming a major character in the set-up of the Bolton team. He scored four goals in the War Cup games, which included two in the regional final against Manchester United in the away leg. He won the Lancashire Cup with Bolton in 1947–48 and was with the club during the time they appeared in three Manchester Cup Finals winning once in 1954. He also played in the FA Cup Final in 1953. In total with other cup and none recorded league games after the war he scored a total of 98 goals. He won three

England caps and represented the Football League on two occasions. During the war he represented the England war side.

He joined Sheffield United in 1956–57 then finished his career as player coach of Wigan Athletic, before becoming the trainer at Hyde United in 1963.

Thomas 'Tommy' Butler was born on the 28 April, 1918 in Atherton and died in 2009 aged 91 years. He played for Bolton during the early war years and more importantly throughout the 1944–45 War Cup run, as a winger. He played in most of the games apart from the national final against Chelsea, when he was replaced by future Bolton Captain Willie Moir. He scored one goal during the Cup campaign and five goals in total for the club. He is only registered with Bolton for league in 1937, though he was a regular member during the latter war years. He is also listed with Oldham Athletic in 1937 then Middlesbrough. In 1946 after the war he is again registered with Oldham and in 1947 appears at Accrington Stanley, who he played 218 games for scoring 26 goals. He finished his career at Wigan Athletic. His brother was twenties legend Billy Butler and his son Dennis played for Bolton in the 1960s before transferring to Rochdale when Bob Stokoe signed him. Before retiring Tommy briefly managed Port Vale.

Tommy Butler

William 'Willie' Moir was born on 19 April, 1922 in Aberdeen and died in May, 1988. He played locally in Scotland and was then in the RAF when the war began. He was spotted by Bolton playing forces football when stationed at Kirkham and joined Bolton an amateur. He was then quickly signed on professional forms in 1943 after guesting for Bolton, Dundee

and Aberdeen. He played in the North/South Final against Chelsea and had scored in the qualifying round against Liverpool and the home semi-final leg with Wolverhampton. Moir was capable of playing anywhere in the forward line, though mostly on the wing before moving to inside-right. Reports state he never stopped running from start to finish of a game. He played 358 registered games and scored 134 goals. Bolton reached the FA Cup semi-final in 1945–46 Moir playing three games with one goal. He won the Lancashire Cup with Bolton in 1948 scoring a hat-trick in the Final. He was with the club when they competed in three Manchester Cup Finals between 1951 and 1954 winning the competition in 1954, 1–0 against Manchester United.

He captained Bolton in the 1953 FA Cup Final against Blackpool scoring one of the goals in the 4–3 defeat. In 1955 he transferred to Stockport County and then became their manager in 1958 until 1960. Willie gained one cap for Scotland against England in 1950. After retirement he assisted on the commercial side for Bolton until his death.

Note: For real enthusiasts if you follow this link you will go to a wonderful old film that highlights football during the war years and in particular Bolton's progress to both the north and national finals: film.britishcouncil.org/the-great-game.

Bolton's regular goal scorers throughout the war years were in the main players like Lofthouse, Hunt and Barrass. Walter Sidebottom had begun to have an influence but he joined the Royal Navy and was unfortunately killed in action. (See Sidebottom section of book). Two other players with significant goal contributions were:

Jim Currier: born in Wednesbury in the West Midlands. He initially played for Cheltenham Town and signed for Bolton 1935–39. He scored 14 goals in 26 games. He then went to Manchester City. He was a centre-forward and his record at City is remarkable.

He scored 69 goals in 75 games, but including the War League his total was 113 games with 94 goals. He scored 47 in season 1940–41 and also achieved 50 goals in just 30 games at one point. He played for Bolton in season 1943–44 and was the clubs top scorer with 17 goals. He was also in the losing Lancashire Cup Final team against Liverpool in 1944 over two legs in which he scored one goal. He was a highly gifted forward who always seemed to find the net with considerable ease.

Clifton 'Cliff' Chadwick was born on 26 January, 1914 in Bolton. He played for Turton, Fleetwood then Oldham Athletic and could play on either wing. He signed for Middlesbrough in 1934 and was with them when the Second World War broke out, playing over 96 games for them with 27 goals. He played for Bolton on a number of occasions between 1940–44 scoring 32 goals. After the war he played for Hull City, Darlington and Stockton, whom he then player managed.

There was no official Football League until season 1946–7 and many players had still been in active service, so the football north and south leagues for first and second division clubs continued, Bolton obviously falling into the northern section. It was termed by the football league as 'A transitional period'. Lower league clubs had a similar set up but with smaller sections.

Many of the players involved in the war cup were participant in these leagues. Bolton had a good final season as well as reaching the semi-final of the FA Cup. They finished third in a very strong group of teams, as displayed.

	p	w	d	l	f	a	w	d	l	f	a	ff	fa	pts
Sheffield United	42	14	3	4	61	29	13	3	5	51	33	112	62	60
Everton	42	14	5	2	58	23	9	4	8	30	31	88	54	55
Bolton Wanderers	42	11	6	4	32	18	9	5	7	35	27	67	45	51
Manchester United	42	13	4	4	61	29	6	7	8	37	33	98	62	49
Sheffield Wed.	42	13	5	3	39	20	7	3	11	28	40	67	60	48
Newcastle United	42	13	4	4	68	27	8	1	12	38	43	106	70	47
Chesterfield	42	9	8	4	29	16	8	4	9	39	33	68	49	46
Barnsley	42	11	5	5	44	33	6	6	9	32	35	76	68	45
Blackpool	42	13	4	4	56	34	5	5	11	38	58	94	92	45
Manchester City	42	12	0	9	43	37	8	4	9	35	38	78	75	44
Liverpool	42	10	5	6	47	36	7	4	10	33	34	80	70	43
Middlesbrough	42	12	2	7	44	43	5	7	9	31	44	75	87	43
Stoke City	42	14	2	5	60	24	4	4	13	28	55	88	79	42
Bradford Park Ave.	42	13	2	6	53	35	4	4	13	18	49	71	84	40
Huddersfield Town	42	13	2	6	50	33	4	2	15	40	56	90	89	38
Burnley	42	9	5	7	42	36	4	5	12	21	48	63	84	36
Grimsby Town	42	8	6	7	32	34	5	3	13	29	55	61	89	35
Sunderland	42	12	2	7	33	27	3	3	15	22	56	55	83	35
Preston North End	42	10	2	9	50	34	4	4	13	20	43	70	77	34
Bury	42	8	6	7	35	35	4	4	13	25	50	60	85	34
Blackburn Rovers	42	7	5	9	31	44	4	2	15	29	67	60	111	29
Leeds United	42	7	4	10	36	42	2	3	16	30	76	66	118	25

WALTER SIDEBOTTOM

Tribute to the loss of a brave and gifted young player

As a supplement to the war years a special mention is given in honour of a man who gave his life for his country during this conflict. Harry Goslin had lost his life for the cause and he is well documented, with special mention in this book. This young man's story is also in need of recognition as he is mentioned only briefly in other books and records regarding his time at Bolton Wanderers.

Walter Sidebottom was signed by Bolton as a seventeen-year-old from Oulton United in Leeds, playing as a winger or inside-forward. He was born on 1 February, 1921 in Hunslet, near Leeds and went to Stourton High School. Whilst playing in the West Riding Cup Final in 1936–37 he was spotted by a Bolton scout. He could, it was said, play just about any role in the forward position equally well. Arsenal had also attended on the day, but he chose to sign for Bolton.

Walter pictured with his school and district honours and after selection to represent Yorkshire to play London.

Prior to joining Bolton he had won a number of honours with his school and the Yorkshire district teams. In fact whilst playing for his school in 1930, they went on win the English schools championship after first disposing of all the Yorkshire sides. They eventually beat London in the Final played at Valley Parade, Bradford. He was the youngest of seven brothers who all played football to a good standard and his brother Harry was in the successful school team with Walter. Harry, who I found living in Leeds, said what a gifted player Walter was, fast and athletic making the game look easy. He has no doubt he would have gone on to be a great player. He also said that even in 1930 he stood out by a mile as the best player on the pitch in that national final and he was only ten.

WANDERERS' PROGRAMME

TEAMS FOR GOOD FRIDAY

BOLTON WANDERERS

GOODALL

HAMLETT CATTERALL

GROSVENOR ITHELL McCORMICK

WOODWARD SINCLAIR CURRIER SIDEBOTTOM JONES (S.)

KICK OFF 3-15

WRIGGLESW'TH PEARSON HULLETT L. BRADBURY BRYANT

WHALLEY CHILTON GIBSON

PORTER WORRALL

BREEDON

MANCHESTER UNITED

Bolton Reserves v Man United, 7 April, 1939

He played initially in Bolton 'A' and reserve sides, making his full debut on 25 February, 1939 against Huddersfield, aged 18 years. The news was proudly published in the *Yorkshire Post* the day before the game. The following season he was pushing to break into the first team as a regular when the league was suspended because of war. The War League formed and Walter got his regular chance in the side. Once in the team it is reported that he bonded well with the other players and scored nine recorded goals in 1939–40, with four in one game against Southport. He was second top scorer that season behind Hunt. In 1940–41 he had scored four goals when he became eligible for conscription into the forces and he joined the Royal Navy. He had already started to make an impact and was considered as one to watch drawing attention from other clubs. His brothers had also been called up and were stationed across Europe. Walter was offered the position of PTI stationed in this country near

Walter with his bride Kathleen on their wedding day 9 October, 1943. Kathleen's brother Fred Pendlebury a staunch Bolton fan was the best man. Walter had by now settled happily to life in the Bolton area.

Rochdale, but he told his mother that he could not live with himself accepting this due to the fact that his brothers were abroad serving their country, so he signed up for full duties. His brother Harry had joined the navy the year before him.

There are various reports on Walter and all in all he seems to have been an outstanding player, highly thought of and who would undoubtedly have gone on to greater things. An article in the *Yorkshire Post* in 2002, quoted an ex-pupil recalling that Walter had revisited his old school after he had first joined the Navy and was already well known as a Bolton player by then. He was given a hero's reception by the school and its students. From the information I have gathered and his pre- war triumphs, I to have no doubt Walter would have become a first class player and a tremendous asset to Bolton Wanderers. He was reported to be one the country's best young prospects, so the thought of him alongside Lofthouse would have been a mouth-watering proposition.

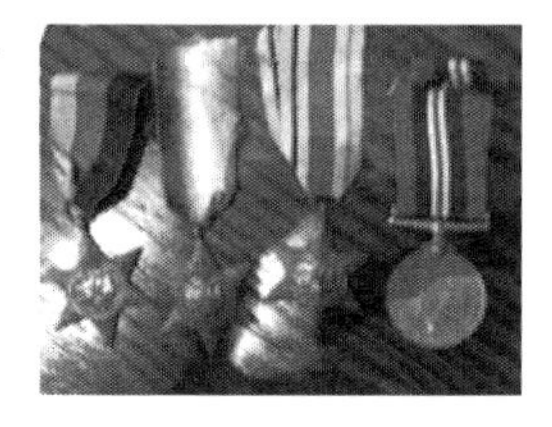

(Note: Harry Sidebottom died in December, 2014 aged 92 years. He had expressed his joy prior to his death at being able to recall fond memories of Walter and their footballing adventures together).

On 23 October, 1943 the ship on which he was serving *HMS Charybdis* was torpedoed in the English Channel and sunk. Walter sadly lost his life aged just 22 though there is no official report as to exactly how he died as his body was not recovered, it was only two weeks after he had married. He has a plaque in Plymouth Naval Memorial Grounds on panel 80.

His wife Kathleen was now pregnant and she had a son in April, 1944 who she named Walter in his honour. Following his death Bolton Wanderers applied to the Football League and presented his widow with a cheque of £150.

It is a sad story and many people may never have heard of him outside of family and friends. I knew the name but only through my research, had he survived I am sure he would have become a household name. By highlighting some of his tragically short career in some brief detail, gives me the satisfaction that it will now allow people to acknowledge him and the sacrifice he and indeed many others made to protect their loved ones and their country. Hopefully this brief passage in the book will make people aware of him as a person and dedicated Bolton Wanderers player. His family are immensely proud of him and I know I am now and I didn't even know him. After researching his story and meeting his relatives, he will be forever etched within my memory.

CLUB SUCCESS 1946–1958

The first season back, with a full FA Cup schedule. Bolton reached the semi-final. A lot of interest following the war and this was the only time FA Cup ties were played over two legs, as there was still no full League schedule. Interest was massive following the war and crowds were large. Bolton dispatched on aggregate, Blackburn Rovers 4–1, Liverpool 5–2 and Middlesbrough 2–1.

In the quarter-final it was Stoke City and over 50,000 watched the away leg which Bolton won 2–0, both goals from Westwood, Stanley Matthews gracing the Stoke side. The return leg was the ill-fated disaster, which due to the terrible injuries and deaths in the crowd was somewhat of an anti-climax ending 0–0, the authorities forcing the teams to finish the tie on the day. No celebration from the players in the circumstances, as this was one of Bolton's darkest days. The official crowd was 65,419, but as we know from reports it's believed over 80,000 where crammed in. (A judicial enquiry followed).

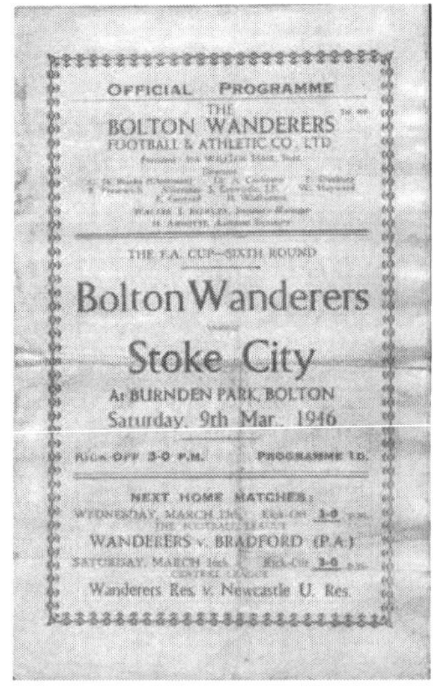

The semi-final only 14 days later on 23 March, 1946 at Villa Park was against Charlton Athletic. Watched by a large crowd of 69,500, Charlton came out on top on the day 2–0. They lost in the Final to Derby County 4–1. Whether the Bolton's player's hearts were in this game after the disaster is questionable, but take nothing away from Charlton, records show they got the result.

Southport: 1948. They have 1 Lancashire Cup win in 1904-5

1. 1947–48 Lancashire Cup winners. At Haig Avenue Southport at this time a Third Division outfit. It was played on 8 May, 1948. The Wanderers were far too strong for them and won by 5–1. Goals: Moir 3, Bradley and Jackson. On route they beat Everton 4–3, Bury 3–2 and Blackburn Rovers 1–0. Team: 1. Hanson 2. Roberts 3. R. Banks 4. Howe 5. Gillies 6. Barrass 7. Woodward 8. Jackson 9. Lofthouse 10. Bradley 11. Moir. This was the last time Bolton won this trophy until 1988.

The future manager Bill Ridding a former Manchester United player before injury finished his career early, is at this time team trainer. Former Bolton 'keeper Bob Jones is pictured back right in the Southport team picture, he was at that time their trainer.

The Trotter magazine became a favourite with the fans and David Jack gave an introductory message in this first issue.

In 1950 Bill Ridding became manager until 1968. Some say he was controlled by the board, but he did remarkably well if he was. He was experienced and had a very knowledgeable backroom staff assisting him, with people like Bert Sprotson, George Taylor and George Hunt to name but three.

A Message from David B. N. Jack

David Jack

TO ALL PATRONS OF "THE TROTTER"

Nothing gives me greater

The Trotter magazine became a favourite with the fans and David Jack gave an introductory message in this first issue.

Lofthouse also spoke highly of him. Until the early 1960s Bolton maintained a very strong position in a competitive Football League with a sound infrastructure. In 1951–52 they finished fifth in the First Division, upcoming future dominant clubs like Manchester United, Tottenham and Arsenal finished top three respectively. Fortunately Bolton still had a very strong team and an excellent development system. This was backed up by a good scouting team.

Bolton moved forward in the 1950s as strong and feared as ever. Teams hated coming to Burnden Park. If the word fear entered into your vocabulary it was said, then don't bother turning up. United and England legend Nobby Stiles said, "If you got tackled at Bolton you knew about it" and Jimmy Greaves said he hated playing Bolton, but they still possessed a lot of quality. Pictured are the 1950 and mid 1950s teams.

Bert Sprotson the trainer was a fine player in his own right. He played for such clubs as Leeds United, Manchester City and Tottenham. He was capped by England 11 times. He is pictured left as a Leeds player and as trainer at Bolton 1952.

2. 1950–51 Bolton won the West Lancashire Cup. (1951–52 team pictured).

3. 1951–52 and 1952–53 in the Manchester Cup they reached the final in both seasons, losing to Bury 2–1 at Gigg Lane and the following season to Oldham Athletic at Boundary Park 3–1.

4. 1953 FA Cup Runners Up. This is probably one of the most publicised finals in the English game. Known as the Matthews Final in Coronation year and because of his exploits in the last twenty minutes. He had been been playing since 1932 without a trophy and this was his only major success.

The Final at Wembley on 2 May, 1953 was before 100,000. Bolton's progress to the Final was Third round, Fulham 3–1, Holden, Moir, and Lofthouse. Fourth round, Notts County

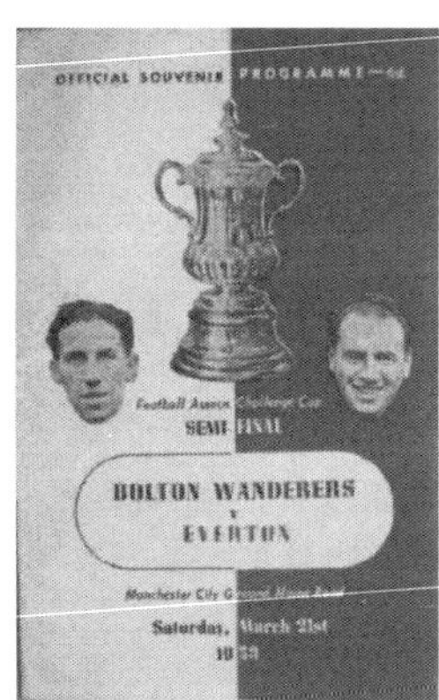

1–1, Lofthouse, 2–2 Moir 2, 1–0, Lofthouse. Fifth round, Luton Town 1–0, Lofthouse. Six round Gateshead 1–0, Lofthouse. The semi-final at Maine Road against Everton 4–3, Lofthouse 2, Moir, Holden before 75,213.

Bolton had led 2–1 at half-time then took a 3–1 lead with goals from Lofthouse, Langton and Bell. Bell had passed himself fit before the game but was carrying a hamstring injury and after just eighteen minutes he was virtually a passenger in the game. He was put out on the wing, leaving Langton and Hassall to cover. Yet he somehow managed to grab the third

Everton FC 1953–44

goal. With 20 minutes to play the extra man was telling and Matthews turned on his magic. Nevertheless Lofthouse, hit the post at 3–1. If that had gone in, even Matthews would not have been able to work his magic Lofthouse later stated. The winning goal came in the ninety-second minute. A game Bolton really should have won, but playing for most of it with ten men finally overcame them physically and don't forget substitutes were not allowed. Lofthouse had now scored in every round, but it was no consolation to him.

Bolton still received a great welcome back from the fans into the town, as seen below.

Blackpool FC 1953

Note: Stanley Matthews FA Cup medal sold at auction in November, 2014 for £220,000 which is a world record. Middle far left is manager, Joe Smith the former Bolton idol and next to him Stan Matthews. In an interview some years later Matthews quoted: "It was an FA Cup medal then that everyone wanted, winning the League was a great achievement but the Cup medal was what they all prized.

Back row—McNulty, Aston, Chilton, Crompton, Jones, Lewis, Byrne, Gibson.
Front row—Berry, Rowley, Taylor, Pearson, Pegg, Cockburn.

5. 1953–54 Manchester Cup winners. At Old Trafford against Manchester United. They won 1–0. Bolton still producing good quality players and teams, as shown in 1955 when the reserves won the Central League for the first time. The youth team also reached the semi-final of the FA Youth Cup in 1956. Bolton had great strength in depth and the beaten Manchester United side was during the upcoming Busby Babes era.

6. 1957–58 FA Cup winners. The team finished the league in the lower half of the table but reached what was again to be another widely publicised Final. Manchester United who had lost eight of their squad in the Munich air disaster, were the opponents. Players like Lofthouse and other team members knew these players well, but said they could not let feelings or sentiment come into it.

Route to the Final.

Bolton 3–0 Preston (Stevens, Parry 2)

Bolton 3–0 York (Birch, Allcock 2)
after 0-–0 draw

Bolton 3–1 Stoke (Lofthouse, Stevens, Parry)

Bolton 2–1 Wolves (Stevens, Parry)

Semi-final (Lofthouse was injured)

Bolton 2–1 Blackburn (Gubbins 2 pictured below) at Maine Road before 74,800.

Blackburn Rovers semi-finalists 1958

This was the side that Bill Ridding later famously quoted cost eleven £10 signing on fees, so effectively winning the FA Cup for £110.

The game was not a spectacle as such and Bolton took an early lead after three minutes through Lofthouse. The second goal after fifty minutes is disputed and Lofthouse admits was a foul. Harry

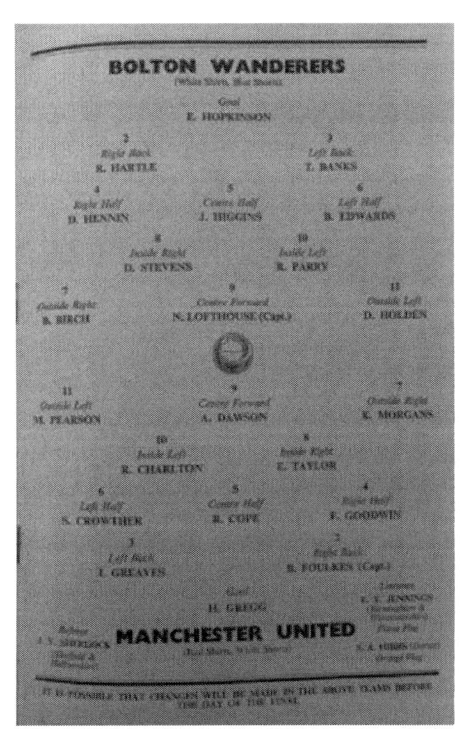

BOLTON WANDERERS

(White Shirts, Blue Shorts)

Goal
E. HOPKINSON

2 *Right Back* R. HARTLE — 3 *Left Back* T. BANKS

4 *Right Half* D. HENNIN — 5 *Centre Half* J. HIGGINS — 6 *Left Half* B. EDWARDS

8 *Inside Right* D. STEVENS — 10 *Inside Left* R. PARRY

7 *Outside Right* B. BIRCH — 9 *Centre Forward* N. LOFTHOUSE (Capt.) — 11 *Outside Left* D. HOLDEN

11 *Outside Left* M. PEARSON — 9 *Centre Forward* A. DAWSON — 7 *Outside Right* K. MORGANS

10 *Inside Left* R. CHARLTON — 8 *Inside Right* E. TAYLOR

6 *Left Half* S. CROWTHER — 5 *Centre Half* R. COPE — 4 *Right Half* F. GOODWIN

3 *Left Back* I. GREAVES — 2 *Right Back* B. FOULKES (Capt.)

Goal
H. GREGG

MANCHESTER UNITED

(Red Shirts, White Shorts)

IT IS POSSIBLE THAT CHANGES WILL BE MADE IN THE ABOVE TEAMS BEFORE THE DAY OF THE FINAL.

Above: goals 1 and 2, then with the Cup

Gregg was bundled into the net, but the goal stood and the cup was secured.

From left, Lofthouse's medal, the actual match ball and his team blazer badge. The ball was initially lost after the game, but after a press appeal it was returned amazingly, by a fan and given to Lofthouse.

Wolves 1958

7. 1958 Charity Shield. Wolves were the opponents captained by Billy Wright the England skipper. They were the League Champions and a quality outfit. Bolton won the game by 4–1 with goals from Hill, Bannister, and Lofthouse (2). Durandt scored late on for Wolves. This showed that on their day Bolton Wanderers were as good as anyone. Attendance: 36,029 at Burnden Park.

Triumphant return to Bolton Town Hall by the 1958 Cup side.

1953 FA Cup Final players:

1. Stan Hansen also spelt Hanson was born in Bootle on 27 December, 1915 and died on 1 January, 1987. He came to Bolton in 1934 as a goalkeeper and stayed his whole career retiring in 1956 after 423 games. He only won his place in the side in 1938 when he displaced Fred Swift, the brother of the famous Manchester City 'keeper Frank. (Frank was killed in the Munich air disaster in 1958 when he was travelling with the Manchester United team as a reporter for the game). After 1956 Stan assisted on the coaching side with the club as well as continuing to play part-time for Rhyl. He also ran a Post Office near to Burnden Park. He was one of 15 Bolton players who famously signed up for the war effort in 1939 and served throughout the whole campaign, though he did play for the armed forces and the Bolton wartime side during the war when available and appeared in the famous FA Cup Final defeat of 1953 against Blackpool.

He won the Lancashire Cup with Bolton in 1938–39, 1947–48, Bolton also won the Manchester Cup in 1937–38 and the West Lancashire Cup in 1950–51 during his time at the club. He reached the FA Cup semi-finals with Bolton in 1945–46. He toured Canada with the FA side of 1950 with Nat Lofthouse. Stan is pictured in action in a game against Wolves, with Gillies and Banks in close attendance.

2. John Ball was born in Ince, Wigan on 13 March, 1925 and joined them prior to the war. He then guested for them and Gravesend during the war years. In 1948 he signed for Manchester United for £2,000 and was an understudy to Johnny Carey. He only made 23 appearances and Bolton secured his services in 1950 as a full-back. He played in the

1953 Final, but was eventually displaced by Roy Hartle who he had beaten to the full-back spot for the Final. He remained in the squad till 1957–58 and filled in at either full-back position. He represented the football league on two occasions. He returned to Wigan in 1958 and then managed the team in 1960–63. On retirement from the game he ran a decorating business and later emigrated to Australia.

3. Ralph Banks was born on 28 June, 1920 in Farnworth and died on 1 October, 1993. He played locally then for South Liverpool signing for Bolton in 1941. He made his debut in the Football North League that year after the club had been closed because of the war. He then served in the North Lancashire regiment till the end of the war and played forces football in the Far East. He was then called up again for National Service, so this greatly affected his career. He still played 118 games for the club, but only played three league games alongside his brother Tommy. He played in the 1953 FA Cup Final and had the dubious honour of trying to mark Stan Matthews, this being his last game for the club. He was with Bolton when they won the Lancashire Cup in 1947–48 and the West Lancashire Cup in 1950–51. In 1954 he transferred to Aldershot then finished his career at Weymouth.

4. John Wheeler was born in Crosby, Liverpool on the 26 July, 1928. He played for Tranmere Rovers and Bill Ridding signed him in 1951 as he had been trainer there. He played 205 games and scored 18 goals for Bolton playing in the 1953 Final. He transferred to Liverpool and played under Bill Shankly playing over 450 games for them. He ended his career at Bury as assistant trainer till after 1969, after turning down the player manager role at New Brighton. He moved into the area with his wife Freda and his three children; he was last known residing in the West Lancashire area.

5. Malcolm Williamson Barrass (His information is contained in the section of the book referring to the War Cup 1945.).

6. Eric Bell was born in Clayton, Manchester on 27 November, 1929 and died on 22 July, 2012 in Wythenshawe. He signed for Bolton in 1950 after being rejected by Manchester United. He played 118 and scored two goals, he famously scored in the 1953 Cup Final with a header whilst playing on one leg. He had declared himself fit for the game but the hamstring went after just 18 minutes and he was virtually a passenger for the rest of the game. It was stated that Bolton played for most of the game without him, even though he scored and this took its toll on the team late in the second half when Matthews began to play his part in Blackpool's comeback. He played for Bolton until 1958 when a knee injury forced his retirement.

He played for England B on two occasions and also represented the Football League. He was with the club when they won the West Lancashire Cup in 1950–51. Matt Busby was quoted; "I have rejected dozens of young amateurs at Old Trafford. I can say that in relation to Eric Bell I misjudged him, though at the time I thought it was the right decision".

7. Douglas Holden was born on 28 September, 1930 in Manchester and played locally before being signed by Bolton in 1948 as an amateur. He made his debut in 1951 as a winger, replacing Bobby Langton and was described as fast with two good feet. He played in the FA Cup Finals of 1953 and 1958. He was at Bolton when they won the West Lancashire Cup in 1950–51. He won five England caps and also represented England Youth and The Football League. Holden played 463 games and scored 44 goals.

He moved to Preston North End in 1962 and reached the FA Cup Final with them scoring a goal in a 3–2 defeat against West Ham. In 1965 he moved to Australia and coached Sydney Hakoah and Auburn. He also played in the Australian national team. In 1970 he returned to England and coached at Grimsby Town before retirement.

8. Willie Moir (is covered in the section of the book relating to the War Years Final.)

9. Nat Lofthouse is covered in the section of the book dedicated to him personally.

10. Harold Hassall was born in Tyldseley on 4 March, 1929. He played locally for colliery sides and was signed by Huddersfield Town in 1946, making his debut in 1948. He was an inside forward and first won England recognition in 1951 playing five times in total with four goals. He signed for Bolton in 1952 for £27,000 and played in the 1953 Cup Final. Harold played 109 games and scored 34 goals. In 1955 in a game against Chelsea at Burnden he seriously injured his knee and his career was over at 25 years of age. Bill Ridding and Bert Sprotson both said they knew at the time when it happened that it was bad and would probably be the end of his footballing career. He was given a benefit and testimonial in 1957 with over 20,000 attending. He was a qualified teacher and gained football coaching badges. He was England youth coach in 1966 and did research work for FIFA. He managed Malaysia in

1969–70 then became a lecturer and lived in the Lostock Hall area of Bolton. Harold died on 30 January, 2015, he was 85 years old.

11. Robert 'Bobby' Langton was born in Burscough on 8 September, 1918 and died on 13 January, 1996. He signed for Blackburn Rovers in 1938 for £50 from Burscough Victoria. He played outside-left and was regarded as very tough. He became their leading scorer but the war interrupted his career, he joined the Infantry and he was then stationed in India. In 1945 whilst still in the services and now in Northern Ireland he secured the Irish Cup with Glentoran. He went to Preston in 1948 and Bolton signed him in 1949 for a record club fee of £20,000. He played 132 games for the club and scored 18 goals playing in the 1953 FA Cup Final. He was then in dispute with Bolton and returned to Blackburn in the same year, before finished his career with Ards in Ireland in 1956–57. He played three seasons in amateur football and was also a publican. He did some scouting for Accrington Stanley then managed Burscough winning the Lancashire Combination and Junior Cup. He retired in 1971. In 1998 two years after his death the road leading past Burscough football ground was renamed Bobby Langton Way in his honour.

Players from the 1958 FA Cup Final and Charity Shield

1. Edward 'Eddie' Hopkinson was born in Durham on 29 October, 1935 and died on 25 April, 2004. His family moved to Royton and he signed from Oldham Athletic aged sixteen in 1951–52. He signed for Bolton in 1952 which Oldham were far from happy about and they blamed Hopkinson for not showing any loyalty at the time, but this was eventually resolved. He completed national service and made his

debut in 1956–57 when Ken Grieves was committed to Lancashire Cricket Club.

He was only 5ft 9in but very athletic and went on to win six under 21 England caps and 14 full caps. He played in the 1958 Cup triumph. Eddie played 578 games for Bolton, a club record and was awarded a testimonial in 1971, in which Eusebio and Simoes played. In 1974 he spent a brief time as assistant at Stockport County then returned to Bolton as a 'keeper coach. He is in the clubs hall of fame.

2. Roy 'Chopper' Hartle was born on 4 October, 1931 in Bromsgrove, West Midlands and died on 5 November, 2014 aged 83 years. He signed as an amateur aged sixteen for the Wanderers and had played for Bromsgrove Rovers, though he had to complete national service. He made his professional debut in 1953 and played in every round of the FA Cup, but was devastated to be left out of the Final for John Ball who had been injured. He gained the full-back position as his own and from 1955 could not be displaced. Roy played in the 1958 FA Cup winning Final team and played 499 games in total (1 as substitute) with 13 goals for Bolton. He was said to be the best full-back never to play for England, though he did play for England B and the Football League side. He was very tough and feared but fair, he was well respected and a complete gentleman off the pitch.

He left Bolton in 1966 and had a brief spell in the Cheshire league before retiring. He then became a Councillor in Bolton and was on the executive PFA. He was also a qualified PFA coach and coached in America when the North American league was formed. He was awarded a testimonial in 1969. He did corporate work for Bolton at the Reebok Stadium, where a lounge is named after him and was inducted into the clubs hall of fame. A book was produced about his football experiences, *The Life of Roy Chopper Hartle*.

3. Tommy Banks was born on 10 November, 1929 in Farnworth. Regarded as one of the original hard men of football. He played locally and signed in 1947 while still working in the pits. He made his debut in 1948 and made the full-back position his own. He regularly put opposition wingers onto the running track around Burnden and along with Roy Hartle sent many a one home with a gift of 'gravel rash'. Though he was still a quality player and won six England caps playing in the 1958 World Cup finals in Sweden and also represented the football league. He won the FA Cup with Bolton in 1958 and played 255 games for Bolton scoring two goals. In 1961 he went on to play in the Cheshire league for Altrincham and finally for Welsh club Bangor, playing in the Welsh Cup Final in 1964. On retirement he went into the building trade in the Farnworth area where he still resides. He is pictured here and also seen getting to grips with Bobby Charlton in the 1958 fFnal. Tommy's biography *Ah'm Tellin' Thee* was published in 2012.

4. Derek Hennin was born on 28 December, 1931 and died in January, 1989. He played for Prescot Cables who were a great outfit who took a lot of players from the likes of Liverpool and Everton who had not quite made the grade. Although amateurs they were allowed to train every day and were a very good side.

He signed for Bolton in 1949 as a centre-half and played for England youth in the same year. It took until 1954 for him to become a Bolton

regular and in that season Bolton finished fourth in the First Division. John Wheeler was his nemesis and he was in the reserve side again in 1955. But Bolton won the Central League that year, again putting him in the spotlight. He became a first team regular again in 1957 and was the quiet unsung hero of the side and one of the most reliable players in the team. A tough resolute player with a no nonsense approach and apparently a real gent from what I have been told. He was part of the 1958 Cup winning side. In 1961 he moved to Chester City then onto Wigan where he ended his career. He played 183 games for Bolton and scored nine goals. He was a family man who just got on with the job in hand.

5. John Higgins was born in Bakewell on 15 November, 1932 and died on 22 April, 2005. The son of a local baker he joined Bolton from Buxton in 1950. He was a big strong player who eventually became a centre-half in the forces during National Service. He was an understudy to Malcolm Barrass and filled the position in 1956 after Barrass left. He played 202 games for the club and other strikers hated playing against him. He transferred in 1960 to Wigan Athletic. In 1963 he played for Altrincham for two seasons and was later general manager of Stockport County in the 1980s. His son Mark another tough centre-half played for Everton, Manchester United, Bury and Stoke.

6. Bryan Edwards was born on 27 October, 1930 in Woodlesford near Leeds. He was an all-round sportsman and excelled at both football and cricket. He was signed when only 17 years of age as a wing-half, making his debut in 1950. He was called up for national service and this affected his career with Bolton and appearances. He was left out of the 1953 FA Cup Final, but was in the side when they won in 1958. He played 518 games and scored nine goals. He retired in 1965 to take on a training role at Blackpool then coached at Preston and Plymouth before managing Bradford City. He then qualified as a physiotherapist and worked at Huddersfield, Leeds United and returned to finish at Bradford performing a number of assistant roles. He was at Bradford when they won the Third Division title in 1984–85, but this was tainted with tragedy as the Valley Parade fire happened on the last day of the season killing 56 people, which seriously affected him. He is pictured on the previous page prior to the 1958 Cup Final.

7. Brian Birch was born in Southport on 9 April, 1938 and played locally for Southport Boys before Bolton signed him aged 16 years as a junior. He played youth football for England and made his Bolton debut in 1954. He played in every round in the year Bolton won the FA Cup. He was then called up to do national service in the RAF. He was eventually displaced by Brian Pilkington signed from Burnley and he left to play for Rochdale in 1964 having played 191 games with 28 goals. He ended his career at Bangor City then Ellesmere Port. He did some coaching and also worked in South Africa. His son Jordan works in Atlanta for Chelsea Academy, his grandson Will Johnson plays abroad in the major soccer league for Portland Timbers and is a Canadian International.

8. Dennis Stevens was born in Dudley on 30 November, 1933 and died on 20 December, 2012. He was signed by Bolton aged just 15 years. He was cousin to Duncan Edwards and made his debut in 1953 and was a main stay in the team after Harold Hassell had to retire in 1955. He was part of the FA Cup side in 1958 and was

Bolton's top scorer in 1959–60. He then moved to Everton in 1962 for £35,000, a then club record for a received fee. He won the league title with Everton in 1963. He had played 310 games and scored 101 goals for Bolton.

He moved to Oldham Athletic in 1965 and Tranmere in 1967. After winning promotion with them in 1968 he had to retire with back problems. He then ran a gent's outfitters in the Harwood area. On 29 September, 2012 before Bolton's home game with Birmingham City a minutes silence was observed in his honour with both sets of fans behaving impeccably.

9. Nat Lofthouse (See his section of book)

10. Raymond Alan 'Ray' Parry was born in Derby on 19 January, 1936 and died on 23 May, 2003. He was only 15 when he played for Bolton and had already represented England Schoolboys aged 14. Both his brothers played league football and he made his Bolton debut in 1951 as an inside-forward. Although a regular in 1953 he did not play in the Cup Final, but was part of the team winning in 1958. He played 299 games and scored 79 goals. In 1960 he moved to Blackpool and then Bury in 1964 until 1972, when he joined New Brighton. He qualified as an FA coach and ran a newsagent's in Bolton. He had won two England caps and Under-23 honours on another two occasions. He died of cancer in 2003.

11. Doug Holden's profile is in the 1953 player's write up. He won the FA Cup with Bolton in 1958.

The Charity Shield match as mentioned earlier was played on 5 October, 1958 at Burnden Park. The team on the day had five changes from the cup final and is now detailed

1. Joseph 'Joe' Dean was born in Manchester on 4 April, 1939 and joined Bolton in 1955 as a junior. His appearances were limited by the ever-present Hopkinson and he only played 17 games. He went to Carlisle United in 1959–60 and played over 153 games for them helping them to the Third Division title in 1965. He then played for Barrow and Stockport County. He had also gained England Youth international schoolboy honours.

2. Gordon Edwards was born on 14 October, 1935 in Wrexham and signed as a junior. He played three games in season 1958–59. He was a half-back and had won Welsh schoolboy honours. There are no league records of him after the 1958–59 season.

3. Malcolm Edwards was born on 25 October, 1939 in Wrexham and was the brother of Gordon. He was also a half-back and had won Welsh schoolboy and U23 honours. He signed as a junior for Bolton in 1956–57 and played 14 games with one goal for the club. In 1960 he transferred to Chester City. He also played for Tranmere, Barrow and finished his career at Bangor City.

4. Neville Bannister seen above was born on 21 July, 1937 in Brierfield, Lancashire. He was predominantly a winger and signed as a junior. He played 26 games and scored four goals. He moved to Lincoln City in 1960 and also played for Hartlepool and Rochdale. He finished his career at Fleetwood in 1970. He moved into the area and coached local junior football.

5. Freddie Hill was born on 17 January, 1940 and joined as a junior in 1957–58, after playing in the Sheffield area. He made his debut in 1958. He played 410 games and scored 79 goals. He was never totally content at the club and made a number of transfer requests. He failed a medical before a move to Liverpool and eventually transferred to Halifax Town in 1969 for £5,000. In 1970 Manchester City signed him for £12,000 after Francis Lee mentioned him to the club. He moved to Peterborough in 1973 before ending his career with Cork Hibernians and in Sweden. He then played local football in the Manchester area. He is listed in the Peterborough Football Club Hall of Fame and was also given a testimonial by Bolton Wanderers. He won honours at U23 level on 10 occasions, won two full England caps and also represented the Football League side.

A special mention: Ralph Gubbins was born on 31 January, 1932 in Ellesmere Port and died on 11 September, 2011. He did not play in the FA Cup Final 1958, but was instrumental in Bolton getting there. He had limited appearances in the side and played 101 games scoring 18 goals. He was signed in 1952 after his military service and played as a winger or centre-forward. He transferred to Hull City in 1959 and also played for Tranmere Rovers and Wigan. He then worked in the newspaper industry after retiring.

His glory for Bolton came in the cup campaign semi-final when Lofthouse was injured, so no pressure there then! He rose to the occasion scoring both goals in a 2–0 victory against Blackburn Rovers. He had the disappointing misfortune to have to sit out the Final as the 12th man, as Lofthouse had regained his fitness.

The lads of 1958 will always be remembered.

THE SPECIAL ONES

1920s Wonderful Wanderers

They called it the 'roaring twenties' and it was undoubtedly this period that put Bolton on the world stage. They were one a select number of top sides to have consistently maintained high standards of football throughout an entire decade. Set in an era when the game of football could still be sometimes tough and extremely physical, though without doubt during the next ten years we most probably saw the best Bolton sides ever produced to date.

Right into the late 1940s newspaper and sports magazines were still enthusiastically writing about Bolton during the 1920s with nothing but the highest of praises. One regular publication entitled *Let's Talk About,* published in 1946 discussed and analysed various teams. It featured an article on Bolton Wanderers and stated. 'I will warrant there isn't a team in football today capable of beating that famous Wanderers team from the FA Cup in 1923, they were simply the greatest of cup fighters. Such brilliance as was displayed by those Bolton men in the 20s is truly phenomenal. '

It was during this period after winning the Manchester Cup in 1920–21, 1921–22 and the Lancashire Cup in 1921–22 alongside third and sixth place finishes in the First Division that a report in the *Athletic News* magazine described them as ' WONDERFUL WANDERERS' and true contenders for the League title. Other speculation was that it was the numerous cup competitions they were involved in that hindered there prospects for the League title and specifically in the FA Cup.

From the 1919–20 campaign until the end of the decade they had two third and fourth place finishes, they also finished sixth twice. People will always say that they did not win the League, but they did win the FA Cup three times in this period, as well as securing the Lancashire Cup on three occasions, the Manchester Cup twice, the Richardson Cup twice and the West Lancashire Cup once. They were also runners up in the Lancashire Cup in 1920–21 and the Manchester Cup 1928–29, a remarkable amount of success and commitment for any club. They are also part of an elite group of teams who have secured three or more wins in FA Cup Finals in a decade. The others are Manchester United, Arsenal, Chelsea, Tottenham, Newcastle, Blackburn Rovers and Wanderers (not Bolton but the London amateur side captained by C.W. Alcock who was the architect for the introduction of the FA Cup competition), the latter two teams being before the turn of the twentieth century.

There had been a period of rebuilding after the First World War when many players had been called up to serve their country. There is also the fact that just prior to the war Bolton had reached the semi-final of the FA Cup in 1914–15, only to lose to the eventual winners Sheffield United 2–1 and as previously stated secured the Lancashire Cup in 1911–12, as well as reaching the Manchester Cup final in 1912–13, so the foundations of a great side were already starting to fall into place pre-war.

The twelve players listed for the 1923 final, Rowley was the 12th man. Joe Smith was Captain. Substitutes were not allowed. (Picture at Burnden Park facing Embankment end.)

Mr Charles Foweraker had taken charge in 1919 and he was instrumental in forming this formidable outfit, which more than held its own with other great teams of the 1920s such as Huddersfield Town, Sheffield Wednesday, Liverpool, Everton, Burnley, Newcastle United and Arsenal. The Wanderers went into every game with the belief that they were going to get some kind of a result, be it home or away, that's how good they were, fearless and others feared them. They attracted crowds of fifty, sixty and seventy thousand and as we know the FA Cup Final of 1923 was estimated to have brought over 200,000 people in and around the Wembley site.

In the main we focus on the teams from the three FA Cup Finals, but other players who played their roles in the League and all other cup winning competitions are also credited. The squad as a whole are given their deserved attention. We start with the 1923 Cup Final:

1. Richard Henry Pym. Born 1893 and died in 1988 aged 95 years, better known as Dick Pym, nickname 'Pincher'. He was from a fishing family in Topsham, Exeter, for whom he also played cricket. He initially played for Exeter City from 1911 as a youth, touring Brazil in 1914 with The Grecians (Exeter City) and they were the first English team Brazil played. He also represented the Southern leagues side. He joined the Devonshire Regiment during the First World War as a PTI and was injured in action two years later after serving with the Surrey Regiment. In 1918–19 he resumed his career with Exeter and signed for Bolton in 1920–21 season for a then record fee of £5,000 for a goalkeeper, making his debut against Preston North

Pym and Blackmore in 1929 and before an Exeter City game in 1983, Pym is on the right in the latter.

End. Exeter City bought their St James' Park ground with the proceeds. He was with Bolton until 1930 and played in all three winning FA Cup Finals during the decade, without conceding a goal in any of them. He was given a benefit match and then played one season at Yeovil before retiring and returning to the family business.

He played a total of 336 games for Bolton and was capped by England on three occasions. He is the longest lived English footballer on records to date.

2. Robert 'Bob' Haworth born 1897 and died 1962 aged 64 years. He was born in Atherton, Bolton. He joined Bolton in 1921 making his debut against West Bromwich Albion and played for them for over ten years, before a broken leg in effect finished his career in a game at Grimsby. He had a brief spell at Accrington before retiring to run a newsagents shop. There is a report that says he was seen in his later years helping out in the tearooms of a local Cooperative Company in the Bolton area. He played 357 games for Bolton, but is not credited with any goals. He had been made captain of the club in 1931 prior to injury. He won three FA Cup winners medals with Bolton.

3. Alex Finney. Born 1892 in St Helens and died 1982 aged 90 years. He was a miner and played local football and at New Brighton before signing in 1922. He was the youngest member of the 1923 Final team. He played 530 games for the club and scored two goals. He did not play for England but did represent the Football League against Ireland in 1928 in a 9–1 win. He was the last player of the 1920s sides to leave the club in 1937 and finished his career where he started at New Brighton. After retiring he worked for the parks department in Wallasey, though did assist another ex-Wanderers player Jack Atkinson in a coaching role.

He won FA Cup medals in 1923 and 1929. He missed the 1926 Final with a serious knee injury.

4. Harry Nuttall. Born 1897 and died 1969 aged 71 years. He was born virtually in Burnden Park itself. His father worked for the club and lived in a cottage, at that time attached to the ground by the embankment end. His brother played for the club and Harry signed in 1920, making his debut against Tottenham in 1921. He played for Bolton until 1932 and after spells at Rochdale and coach at Nelson he returned to work for the club as a trainer and coach. He remained with the club in one capacity or another until 1964, finishing up as kit man. He had Bolton Wanderers written right through him.

He made 326 appearances and scored six goals. He played for England three times and won three FA Cup medals with Bolton.

Nuttall above and his gold watch; presented to all the Bolton players after the 1923 Final as payment bonuses were limited. In 1926 they received cutlery and 1929 clocks.

5. James 'Jimmy' Seddon. Born 1895 and died 1971 aged 76 years. Born in Bolton and played locally, before signing for the club in 1913, making his debut against Middlesbrough in 1914. His career was interrupted by the war and he served in France where he contracted trench

France v England 1923. Result 1–4. Seddon is fifth from the left.

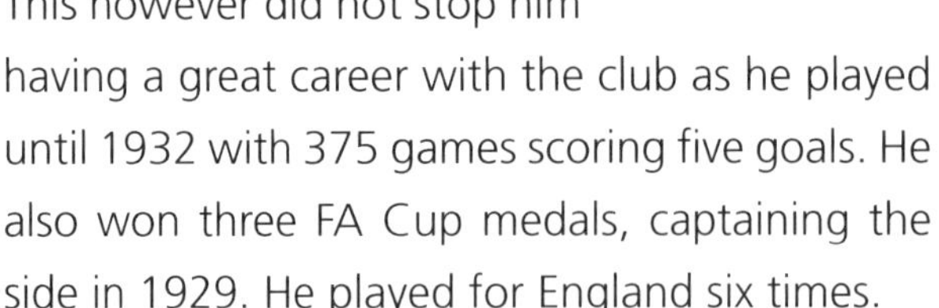

foot, which affected him for the rest of his life, though he signed professionally in 1919. This however did not stop him having a great career with the club as he played until 1932 with 375 games scoring five goals. He also won three FA Cup medals, captaining the side in 1929. He played for England six times.

After leaving the club he coached in Holland and England, specifically at Liverpool and finished up away from football as the manager of the Scarisbrick Hotel, Lord Street, Southport, Lancashire.Seddon at Burnden and in action. One of the main characteristics of Seddon, when he jumped to head the ball, was that he never seemed to raise his arms though he always gained good height.

6. William 'Billy' Jennings. Born 1893 and died 1968 aged 75 years. He was from Barry in Wales and was signed from them in 1912, making his debut in November that year against Derby County.

He initially played at full-back, but was better known for his performances as a half-back once he became established in the side. He was capped by Wales in 1914 and won 11 caps. He served in the Flying Corps during the war. He was plagued by injuries but still managed to regain his place when fit and was a valued member of the 1923 Cup squad and a highly regarded player. He played in the 1923 and

1926 Finals. He made 287 appearances and scored two goals for the club. He played his last game in 1929 and retired in 1931. After this he coached at Notts County and managed Cardiff City from 1937 to 1939 through a troubled financial period.

7. William 'Billy' Butler. Born 1900 and died 1966 aged 66 years, in Durban, South Africa. He was from Atherton and was spotted playing for them, signing for Bolton in 1920. He initially played at centre-forward but switched to the right-wing for the club and became an outstanding player in this role. He played 449 games and scored 74 goals. He was capped by England on one occasion in 1924. He won all three Cup winners medals with the club and scored the opening goal in the 1929 Final.

In 1933 he was transferred at his own request as Bolton had been relegated and joined his former teammate Joe Smith at Reading, who was the manager. He became manager of the club in 1935 after Smith left to manage Blackpool. He was a Physical Training Instructor during the Second World War. In 1945 he emigrated to South Africa where he continued in management and coaching. He is credited with discovering Eddie Stuart of Wolves and Billy Perry of Blackpool during this time.

8. David 'Bone' Nightingale Jack. Born 3 April, 1898 in Bolton. He is probably the most publicised player of this period. Born in Bolton but moved to the Plymouth area with his parents in 1903, as his father Bob Jack became player

Pictured are Bob Jack, David Jack and Rollo Jack

Jacks 1923 medal sold for £15000

manager there. Bob had also played for Bolton between 1895 and 1901. Both his other sons Rollo and Donald signed for Bolton. Jack was also a fine athlete and hurdler. He assisted Chelsea during the war then signed for Plymouth before transferring to the Wanderers in 1920 for £3,500, ahead of the chase by Chelsea and Arsenal. He made his debut against Oldham Athletic. He formed a lethal striking partnership with Joe Smith and played 324 games scoring 161 goals, winning Cup medals in 1923 and 1926. He is immortalised scoring the first ever goal at Wembley against West Ham and he also scored the only goal in the 1926 Final. He won 9 England caps with 3 goals, captaining them 4 times. He represented the Football League on three occasions. In 1928 Bolton reluctantly sold him to Arsenal for £10,890 a world record fee, double the previous record. Herbert Chapman got the Bolton officials drunk and later stated; "They could have got a lot more, the best deal I ever did". Jack then continued a great career with Arsenal winning three league titles and another FA Cup winner's medal. He scored 124 goals in 208 games for the club and in 1934 he began management at Southend, then Middlesbrough and Shelbourne before retiring in 1955 to sports journalist work. He also worked for the Air Ministry and did some scouting for Southend United. He had suffered from ill health from the late 1940s and passed away at the age of 59 on 10 September, 1958 from cancer. He is buried in Streatham Park Cemetery.

9. John Reid Smith. Born 1895 and died 1946 aged 51 years. He was from Pollockshaws, Glasgow, Scotland and joined Bolton from Glasgow Rangers in 1923 for £3,000. He was signed to fill the gap left by Frank Roberts who went to Manchester City in that year. He won the Scottish

Cup prior to this with Kilmarnock in 1920. His debut was a spectacular affair scoring the second goal in the 1923 FA Cup Final. In season 1924–25 he scored 21 goals in 35 games. He won a second FA Cup medal in 1926. In 1928 he was sold to Bury after Harold Blackmore and Jim McClelland were signed. An oversight perhaps as he went on to score 108 goals in 157 games for them, scoring a hat-trick on his debut. He finished his career at Rochdale and Ashton National. After retiring in 1939 he went to work for Bill Jennings as his assistant at Cardiff City. His statistics for Bolton were 174 games and 87 goals.

10. Joseph 'Joe' Smith. Born 1889 and died 1971 aged 82 years. He was from Dudley, West Midlands and was a lethal goal scorer. He started with local side Newcastle St Luke's then went to Crewe but did not play for them joining Bolton in 1908, making his debut against West Bromwich Albion in 1909. He quickly gained a reputation as a prolific scorer and regularly finished as the clubs top marksman at the end of each season. He scored 38 goals in season 1920–21, which is still a club record to this day. The total number of games played that season was 43, including the FA Cup. In one game he scored four goals against Sunderland in a 6–2 home win. During the war he served in the RAF and in 51 wartime games scored 48 goals. He played in the London v Lancashire Final for the London side in 1918, helping them to victory with fellow Bolton team mate Ted Vizard also in the team.

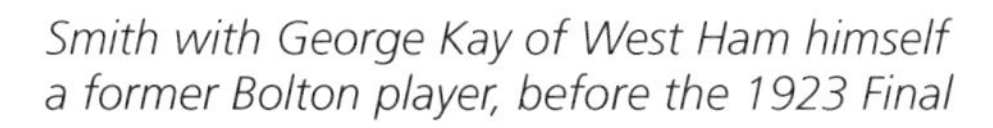

Smith with George Kay of West Ham himself a former Bolton player, before the 1923 Final

Smith pictured in England shirt

He played 492 games for the club and scored 277 goals. He captained the side from the early 1920s until leaving in 1927. He won FA Cup medals in 1923 and 1926. Smith was capped by England in 1913 and gained five in total, but for the war he would undoubtedly have gained others. He had a further eight unofficial game caps for England.

He then played for Stockport from 1927–29 scoring 61 goals in 70 games, finishing his main career with Darwen as player manager scoring 42 goals in 51 games, winning the Lancashire Combination. From 1931 to 1935 he was manager of Reading and then moved to manage Blackpool where he remained in charge until 1958. They gained promotion to the First Division in 1937. As fate would have it he was in charge when they defeated Bolton in the famous 1953 Final. He also took them to FA Cup finals in 1948 and 1951, but they lost on both occasions. Blackpool were also runners up in the First Division in 1955–56. He retired due to ill health in 1958 and was given a golden handshake by Blackpool, who also bought him a house in the town where he lived until his death.

His record speaks for itself and he was highly respected by everyone. Stanley Matthews played for him from 1947 until Smith retired and re-ignited his career, which Matthews credits him with.

11. Edward 'Ted' Vizard, the Welsh Wizard. Born 7 June, 1889 and died in 1973 aged 84 years. From Cogan in Wales he came to Bolton in 1910 on trial and was snapped up immediately, staying for the rest of his career. He made his debut in November against Gainsborough. His career was interrupted by the war and he served in the RAF with Joe Smith. They both guested for Chelsea. They had a great understanding of each other and were a tremendous asset to Bolton. He played 512 games for the club scoring 70 goals, though he is credited with many assists and was later described as George Best like and faster than lightning. He played for the club until 1931 when he was 41 years old, making him the clubs oldest outfield player. He won 2 FA Cup medals with Bolton. After retiring he ran the clubs A team.

He was capped by Wales in 1911 and won 22 caps. He managed Swindon from 1933 then QPR during the World War. His last full position was as Wolves manager from 1944 to 1947. He was replaced by Stan Cullis in 1948, even after finishing third in the League. He retired fully from the game and ran The Mount Hotel in Tettenhall, Wolverhampton prior to his death.

12. Walter Rowley. Born April and died 1976 aged 85 years. He was from Little Hulton and played local football before signing for Oldham Athletic around 1910. He joined Bolton in 1912 making his debut in 1913 against West Brom as centre-half. He was adaptable and could play in any of the half-back roles. During the First World War he continued playing and guested for Port Vale.

He made 191 appearances and scored seven goals. He missed the 1923 Final as he had been suspended for six weeks after being sent off, so he had to be content with being named as the twelfth man for the game. Injury forced his retirement in 1925 and he joined the coaching staff, where he continued in the role during the war. He was a Lancashire Cup winner in 1921–22. He took over as manager in 1944 when illness forced Mr Foweraker to retire. The club won the War Cup North and the overall North, South Final under his management, against

Manchester United and Chelsea respectively. They also reached the semi-final of the FA Cup in 1946 and won the Lancashire Cup in 1947–48. He retired through ill health in 1950, but returned to the game in 1952 and 1955 for spells as manager of Middlesbrough and Shrewsbury Town. He then again retired in the Shrewsbury area through ill health. He was later given a life membership of Bolton Wanderers for 37 years of service to the club.

Harry Woodgate Greenhalgh. The FA Cup Final of 1926 came round and the winning team more or less picked itself. The same players were again in attendance apart from Alex Finney, who had as previously mentioned a knee injury. In stepped Greenhalgh a full back, born 1900 now aged 26 years. He was from Bolton and had played locally for Chorley Old Road Congregational and Atherton. He signed for Bolton in 1924 and played for the club until 1928 playing 80 games. He had not played professionally prior to signing and replaced Bob Haworth who was injured at that time. He was part of the Lancashire Cup Final winning teams of 1924–25 and 1926–27, so when he left the club in 1928–29 it was with some considerable merit. He broke his leg in this season in a game at Derby and that finished his professional career. On retirement he resided in the Bury area until his death in 1982.

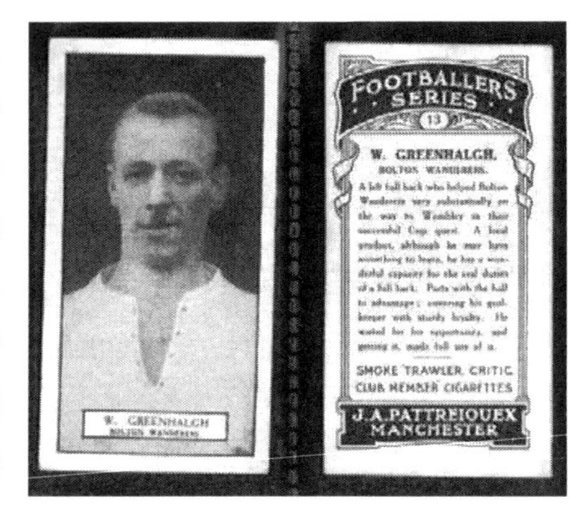

By 1929 some of the players were getting long in the tooth, others had retired, moved on or been sold, such as the two Smiths and Vizard, David Jack was now at Arsenal. Bolton had not stood still though and they bought wisely with funds received to keep up the pressure on the other top sides.

Still playing and in their third FA Cup Final were Pym, Haworth, Seddon now the captain, Nuttall and Butler. Finney was making his second final appearance. From 1927–28 a number of new faces appeared and the following players were in the Final against Portsmouth in 1929.

Fred Kean. Born 1898 in Sheffield and died 1973 aged 74 years in Sheffield. He began his career with Sheffield Wednesday in 1920 and was signed from them in 1928 for £5,600 playing for the club until 1931, making 89 appearances scoring one goal. He was a right-half and won nine England caps, captaining them on one occasion in 1927. In 1931 he moved on to Luton Town until he retired in 1934. He later moved back to his hometown prior to his death. Right, Kean plus team photo after the 1929 Final. (Kean front left lying on the grass)

James 'Jimmy' McClelland. Born 1903 in Dysart, Kirkcaldy, Scotland. He is believed to have begun his career at Rosslyn Park and then Raith Rovers. He was a much travelled player also signed by Southend United, Middlesbrough, Preston, Blackpool, Bradford Park Avenue and Manchester United. He played for Bolton between 1927–30 playing 65 games and scoring 19 goals. He won an FA Cup medal in 1929. He cost Bolton £6,300 from Middlesbrough in 1928, he had scored five goals in a match against Leeds for them. He ended his career at Manchester United in 1936 after they won the First Division title and then held a coaching role there until the outbreak of the Second World War.

Harold Alfred Blackmore. Born 1904 and died 1989. He was born in Silverton, Devon and initially played for Exeter City. Bolton paid £2,150 for his services in 1927 and made his debut against Sheffield Wednesday. He was a prolific goal scorer and was a great replacement for Joe Smith. A very hard role to live up to, but he did a great job for the club. During 1928–29 he scored 30 goals in 35 games. He was the regular top scorer until the arrival of Jack Milsom. He played 165 games for the Wanderers and scored a superb count of 122 goals. In anyone's eyes a tremendous achievement. He scored the second goal in the 1929 Final to put him into the annals of history for Bolton Wanderers. After the arrival of Milsom, he was eventually edged out as age was against him and he moved to Middlesbrough. He then played for Bradford Park Avenue with fellow Cup hero Jim McClelland, before transferring to his last club Bury. After retirement he moved back to Devon and ran a butchers business. Both he and Dick Pym followed the fortunes of Exeter City.

Blackmore pictured at Burnden and the whole squad seen with local dignitaries after the 1929 win. Everyone wanted a piece of them at this time. They were as popular as film stars, without the wages!!

George Bennett Gibson was born 1907 in Hamilton, Scotland. He started his career at Dundee and then moved to Hamilton Academical, where his brother was a member of the board. Bolton signed him in 1926 for £4,100, his brother becoming a useful contact with the club. He played 255 games and scored 81 goals playing mostly as an inside-forward. From 1931 he was regularly given the honour of captaining the club, but this was taken from him with the arrival of Thomas Percival Griffiths from Everton in the same year. He won the FA and 2 Lanc's Cups with Bolton.

Seen above and the 1929 Bolton team with Mr Foweraker and long serving trainer George Eccles. Gibson moved to Chelsea in 1933 and played there until 1939 playing 143 games with 23 goals.

William Lawrence 'Willie' Cook. Born 1906 and died 1981 aged 75 years. He began his career with Forfar and Dundee before signing for Bolton in 1928 for £5,000 making his debut against Leicester City. He was on outside-left and an excellent user of the ball. He was capped by Scotland on three occasions and also represented the Scottish League twice. He won in the FA Cup with the 1929 team and won two Lancashire Cups with Bolton playing 262 games with 40 goals. He transferred to Blackpool in 1936 after helping Bolton return to the First Division. He then won promotion with Blackpool before moving to Reading. In 1938 he returned to Scotland playing for Dundee FC. He also played for Dundee United and during the war assisted the campaign in the RAF. On his retirement he became a licensee in the Dundee area.

These are the main players involved in the various Cup winning sides of the decade, but the squad as a whole were performing heroically in the League and other Cup competitions and a number of other players also earned good reputations within the club and drew considerable interest from other teams requiring their services. Others of note involved in the League and detailed Cup successes are now listed.

Frank Roberts. Born 1893 and died 1961 aged 68 years. He was from Cheshire and played for Sandbach and Crewe. He was signed for £200 in 1914 and led the attack with Joe Smith. Bolton reached the semi-final of the FA Cup in the same year. The forward line of Roberts, Joe Smith, Jack and Vizard was once described as the most potent in the game of football. Unfortunately this all went wrong for Roberts in his final season there, when he took ownership of a hotel in the town, which was against League policy. He was suspended and then transferred to Manchester City for £3,400. After leaving he faced his old teammates in the FA Cup Final in 1926, fortunately for Bolton on the losing side. He played 237 games for City and scored 130 goals. He won four England caps and scored two goals. He later played for Manchester Central and Horwich RMI, before retiring to take up full time trade as licensee of the Victoria Hotel, Bolton. He had won the Lancashire Cup with both clubs.

John Lewis Mansfield Jones. Born 1900 in Abergele. Signed for Bolton in 1922 and took part in the 1922–23 season mainly in the League and Lancashire Cup, scoring three goals. He was part of the FA Cup squad for 1923. In 1926 he moved to Chesterfield Football Club. He only played 15 recorded games for Bolton but was a vital squad member that season; he is pictured in the advert for the Final, right.

Walter John 'Billy' Baggett. Born 1902 and died 1978 aged 76 years. He was from Towcester, Northampton. He joined Wolves in 1922 but did not play for them, moving to Bolton in 1923. He made 27 appearances as an inside-forward scoring 11 goals. He was part of the cup campaign in 1926 and scored one of the goals in the semi-final against Swansea in a 3–0 win. This was his best season with the club. Reports say he was devastated at being left out for the Final and David Jack who felt strongly about the issue, had spoken up for him to play. He was transferred to Reading in the 1926–27 season. He later coached in Greece from the 1930s and it is believed that he evaded capture by the Germans in 1941. He retired to Barrow in 1954 and coached there, where he was known as Gentleman Jack. He was buried in the town. (Pictured seated fourth from left, front row).

Thomas Murray 'Tom' Buchan. Born 1889 and died 1952. He was born in Plumstead, London and started his career at Sunderland, playing minor roles at a number of other clubs. He joined Bolton in 1914 and captained the side during the war whilst working in a munitions factory. He played 117 games and scored 14 goals for the club playing in every position, but usually at inside-left or right. His brother John also played for Bolton, though his other more famous brother Charles Buchan played for Sunderland and Arsenal and won a military medal in the First World War. He is also famed for the football magazines *Charles Buchan Monthly* and *Annual*. Tom won the Lancashire Cup with Bolton in 1920–21. In 1923 he moved on a free transfer to Tranmere Rovers with

ex-Wanderer Harold Hilton. He later played for Runcorn and Atherton before retiring.

William 'Billy' McKay. Born 1906 and died 1977 aged 70 years. He was from West Benhar, North Lanarkshire. He played in Scotland for East Stirling and Hamilton Academical. He moved to Bolton in 1929 for £4,150. He played at wing-half or inside-forward, making 109 appearances for Bolton scoring 19 goals. He was signed to bolster the ageing side and to inject some new life into the team. He won the Lancashire Cup with Bolton in 1931–32, scoring one of the goals in a 3–2 win over Manchester City. He was also in the side when they lost in the same competition to Liverpool the following year. He was transferred to Manchester United in 1934 and won the Second Division title with them. He played 182 games for United scoring 15 goals, though his career was interrupted by the war and he left them in 1946 for Stalybridge Celtic where he finished his career.

John William Cope. Born 1899 and died 1979 aged 79 years. He was from Milton, Staffordshire and began his career at Leek Alexandra signing for Bolton in 1925, as a right–back or centre–half. He played 86 games for the club, playing in the winning Lancashire Cup Final side in 1926–27. Bolton won the FA Cup twice during his time there, but he could not secure a place in either Final. He was transferred to Port Vale in 1929 and helped them secure the Third Division title 1929–30. He left them in 1934 but returned as a trainer

then backroom staff assistant in 1947 and remained with them until he was 76 years old in 1976. He is seen in the Bolton team photo of 1926 in this book, top left back row and in the Port Vale picture during their stated league triumph.

Joseph 'Joe' Cassidy. Born 1896 died 1949 aged 52 years. From Govan, Scotland and played mainly for Celtic, where he had a great scoring record of 104 goals in 204 games where he was revered by the fans, which is one of the reasons Bolton signed him in 1924 for £4,500. He won the military medal in the first war and was nicknamed 'Trooper Joe'. Unfortunately he did not really settle at Bolton and only played 22 games scoring seven goals, which is quite sad really as he could have potentially been a great asset to the club. He did however play in the winning Lancashire Cup side of 1924–25 against Blackpool. He played for a number of other clubs including Cardiff, Dundee, Clyde, Ballymena, Morton and Dundalk. He played for Scotland four times and represented the Scottish League three times.

Bruce Longworth. Born 1898 in Lanchester, Durham and died 1955 in Cornwall. He started at Hopley All Blacks and signed for Bolton in 1919 as a right-half playing 82 games, before moving to Sheffield United in 1924. Like many of the other players he was part of a squad that played many games and was obviously good enough to get his fair share of picks with a very talented bunch of players, throughout the gruelling seasons. He played in the Lancashire Cup Final in 1920–211 and 1921–22 gaining a losers and winners medal. After retiring he became an hotelier and was a member of the Cornish FA. Pictured is his winners Lancashire Cup medal.

William 'Bill' Frederick Weston Hinton. Born 1895 and died 1976 aged 80–81. He was a goalkeeper from Swindon, which was his first club and he moved to Bolton in 1920 until 1924 and played 36 games. He

then went to Tottenham Hotspur. He was unfortunate to be playing at the same time as Dick Pym and became a reserve 'keeper in essence, which was one of the reasons he went to Spurs. He did suffer from ill health and after moving back to Swindon in 1928 had to retire from the game. He then ran timber and box making businesses. He retired to Branksome, Dorset where he lived with his wife Agnes, but was quite ill in later life; his right leg was amputated in 1971 before his death.

He was the 'keeper in the losing 1920–21 Lancashire Cup Final.

Herbert 'Bert' Baverstock. Born 1883 and died 1951 aged 68 years. He was from Dudley, West Midlands, playing there locally before joining Bolton in 1905 and played for the club until 1922. He was described as 'A dogged outstanding defender, an unassuming and dedicated craftsman the sheet anchor to the side.' During the first war he served with the Royal Flying Corps. He played either full-back position but excelled on the right. He played 388 games for Bolton and scored four goals.

He won a Lancashire Cup winners medal in 1911–12 and was in the FA Cup semi-final team of 1914–15. He got a runner up medal for the Lancashire Cup in 1920–21, before moving to Blackpool where he finished his career. He helped Bolton secure promotion from the Second Division on two occasions, in 1908–09 and 1910–11. On retiring he ran the Lever Arms Pub in Bolton.

James Hodson. Born in Wigan and played for Bolton from 1919–21. Little is known about James and he only played 22 games for the club. Prior to joining Bolton he played for Garswood Hall. Regardless of the lack of information on his career he rightfully gets his mention as a squad member of the 1920–21 Lancashire Cup campaign and appearance in the Final.

Herbert Redvers 'Bert' Cartman. Born 1900 and died 1955 aged 55 years. From Bolton and started his career at Waterloo Temperance before signing for Bolton in 1919 and played for them until 1921, when he was transferred to Manchester United. He only played three games for them before going to Tranmere Rovers in 1923, playing 217 games with 32 goals. In 1929 he moved to Chorley where he ended his career. He played 22 games for Bolton and played outside-left or right. He is pictured above and played in the Lancashire Cup Final 1921.

James 'Jimmy' Jones. Born 1889 at Newburn, Tyne and Wear. Initially he played for Gateshead then Blackpool from 1912 to 1919, playing 113 games. He came to Bolton then until 1922, before moving to New Brighton in 1923 where he finished his career in 1927 after playing 141 games for them. He was a left-back playing 70 games for the Wanderers which included the Lancashire Final in 1920–21.

Henry James Boston was born in Nantwich on 20 October, 1899 and died in 1973. He was a winger and signed for Bolton in 1923 from Nantwich Town for £200 playing 39 games with three goals. He was part of the 1926 FA Cup campaign and scored one goal in the third round 6–2 replay win against Bournemouth. He found it difficult to get into the side and was transferred to West Brom in 1929 for £2,000. He played 27 games and scored six goals for them. He then spent a short time at Swansea before finishing his career back at Nantwich, helping them to the Cheshire Cup Final win in 1933 scoring the only goal. Pictured at Bolton 1926 and front left in the Nantwich team.

Honours won during the squad member careers with Bolton Wanderers excluding FA Cup:

1. Dick Pym; 3 Lancashire Cup, 2 Manchester Cup, 1 Richardson Cup.
2. Bob Haworth; 1 Lancashire Cup, 2 Manchester Cup, 1 Richardson Cup, 1 West Lancashire Cup.
3. Alex Finney; 3 Lancashire Cup, 1 Manchester Cup, 2 Richardson Cup, 1 West Lancashire Cup.
4. Harry Nuttall; 2 Lancashire Cup, 2 Manchester Cup, 2 Richardson Cup, I West Lancashire Cup.
5. Jimmy Seddon; 3 Lancashire Cup, 2 Manchester Cup, 2 Richardson Cup, 1 West Lancashire Cup.
6. Bill Jennings; 1 Lancashire Cup, 2 Manchester Cup, 1 Richardson Cup.
7. Billy Butler; 4 Lancashire Cup, 2 Manchester Cup, 2 Richardson Cup, 1 West Lancashire Cup.
8. David Jack; 3 Lancashire Cup, 2 Manchester Cup.
9. Joe Smith; 4 Lancashire Cup, 3 Manchester Cup.
10. Ted Vizard; 4 Lancashire Cup, 2 Manchester Cup, 2 Richardson Cup, 1 West Lancashire Cup.
11. Walter Rowley; 1 Lancashire Cup, 2 Manchester Cup.
12. Harry Greenhalgh; 2 Lancashire Cup.
13. Fred Kean; 2 Richardson Cup, 1 West Lancashire Cup.
14. Jim McClelland; 2 Richardson Cup, 1 West Lancashire Cup.
15. Harold Blackmore; 2 Richardson Cup, 1 West Lancashire Cup.
16. George Gibson; 2 Lancashire Cup, 2 Richardson Cup, 1 West Lancashire Cup.
17. Willie Cook; 2 Lancashire Cup, 2 Richardson Cup, 1 West Lancashire Cup.
18. Tom Buchan; 1 Lancashire Cup, 2 Manchester Cup.
19. Bill McKay; 1 Lancashire Cup, 2 Richardson Cup, 1 West Lancashire Cup.
20. Bill Cope; 1 Lancashire Cup.
21. Joe Cassidy; 1 Lancashire Cup.
22. Bruce Longworth; 1 Lancashire Cup.
23. Bert Baverstock; 1 Lancashire Cup.

THE DEDICATED TRAINER

George Samuel Eccles was born in Newcastle-under-Lyme on 1 January, 1873 according to Everton records and died on 18 December, 1945. He was a right–back and began his main career at Port Vale in 1893 then played for Wolves, Everton, Preston and West Ham. He came to Bolton in season 1904–05 and helped them win promotion back into the First Division, he had six recorded games. He then became a trainer with the club and served them for over twenty years. He worked under Charles Foweraker throughout the whole of the successful 1920s period. He is seen in a number of the team pictures in this book from the mid 1900s up to 1929. He was given a benefit year in 1921. He is seen back left with the Cup side of 1923 and on his benefit year match ticket. He was awarded a medal by the club for services in 1930. Bob Young took over in 1931 and George worked with the reserves part time due to poor health. When Young left in 1941 George again took up the coach's role and assisted in the development of Nat Lofthouse. By all accounts a man full of knowledge and a loyal member of the Bolton staff who quietly went about his job in a totally professional manner, a team member who Mr Foweraker was reliant upon and trusted completely.

The 1920s in my humble opinion was Bolton's best ever competing squad of players throughout its entire history. I am more than convinced that there is also a good argument that they were rivals to match Huddersfield Town as one of the country's top sides during that period, as they more than matched them and the best teams in competitive encounters,

George Eccles' Benefit.
BURNDEN PARK.
Wednesday, April 27th, 1921.
Kick-off 6-30 p.m.
Bolton Wanderers
(Full team)
v.
11 Internationals.
Tickets 1/-

though you could say Huddersfield showed more consistency as seen by their league triumphs. As a Cup and impact club though there was none better than Bolton, they knocked Huddersfield out of the FA Cup during their 1923 and 1929 campaigns. Bolton Wanderers were a team that were hugely admired and the North in footballing terms was also the stronghold for football and Bolton was quoted as: 'a team full of skill', which made their successes in the Lancashire and Manchester cups even more special. Two statistics that back the facts that northern England contained the best sides are: that until 1930 no team further south than the midlands had ever secured the League One title and only Tottenham Hotspur had won the FA Cup after 1900. The team that then broke that duck was Arsenal and they had secured the services of one David Jack from Bolton Wanderers to assist them in achieving both.

Notes: Huddersfield Town pictured: League record 1920 to 1930. Three League titles, 1924, 1925 and 1926. Two second and one third place finish. FA Cup winners 1921–22, runners up 1920, 1928 and 1930. From 1921–25 their manager was the famous Herbert Chapman, who then went onto manage Arsenal with similar success. Bolton consistently matched them in head-to-heads throughout the decade, though any argument put aside they are both true greats in football history.

BOLTON WANDERERS:

Tour results up to 1940.

(Note particular reference to the 1920s)

Tour of 1909

16-5-1909	Den Haag	Haagsche BS-Bolton Wanderers	1-4 W
20-5-1909	Rotterdam	Sparta Rotterdam-Bolton Wanderers	0-3 W
23-5-1909	Rotterdam	Zwaluwen Rotterdam-Bolton Wanderers	0-6 W
30–5-1909	Amsterdam	Amsterdam-AFC-Bolton Wanderers	1-8 W
01-6-1909	Dordrecht	Dordrecht-FC-Bolton Wanderers	1-10 W

Tour of 1913

01-5-1913	Duisburg	Duisburg SV-Bolton Wanderers	1-5 W
04-5-1913	Berlin	Berliner TuFC Viktoria-Bolton Wanderers	2-1 L
11-5-1913	Wien	Wiener Athletic Club-Bolton Wanderers	0-3 W
12-5-1913	Wien	Wiener Sport Club-Bolton Wanderers	0-3 W
15-5-1913	Wien	SK Rapid Wien-Bolton Wanderers	3-3 D
16-5-1913	Wien	FK Wiener Amateure-Bolton Wanderers	2-2 D
18-5-1913		Deutsche Association-Bolton Wanderers	0-12 W

Tour of 1923

20-5-1923	Genéve	FC Servette Genéve-Bolton Wanderers	2-2 D
21-5-1923	Bern	Young Boys Bern-Bolton Wanderers	0-2 W
23-5-1923	Basel	Nordstern Basel-Bolton Wanderers	1-2 W
26-5-1923	La Chaux	FC La Chaux-de-Fonds-Bolton Wanderers	0-5 W
27-5-1923	Zürich	Select Zürich-Bolton Wanderers	1-5 W
30-5-1923	Bern	Young Boys Bern-Bolton Wanderers	1-2 W
02-6-1923	Mulhouse	Mulhouse FC-Bolton Wanderers	0-6 W
03-6-1923	Strasbourg	Select Alsace-Bolton Wanderers	0-3 W

June, 1923 before the game against Mulhouse in the Alsace region, France. Bolton won 6–0

Tour of 1924

04-5-1924	Dresden	DSV Guts Muts-Bolton Wanderers	1-3	W
07-5-1924	Leipzig	Fortuna Leipzig-Bolton Wanderers	0-9	W
11-5-1924	Praha	AC Sparta Praha-Bolton Wanderers	1-3	W
13-5-1924	Nürnberg	1 FC Nürnberg-Bolton Wanderers	0-4	W
15-5-1924	München	FC Bayern München-Bolton Wanderers	1-3	W
18-5-1924	Berlin	TuFC Union Berlin-Bolton Wanderers	0-4	W
19-5-1924	Leipzig	Aberdeen FC-Bolton Wanderers	1-3	W
21-5-1924	Amsterdam	Ajax FC Amsterdam-Bolton Wanderers	1-3	W
25-5-1924	Amsterdam	Leeds United-Bolton Wanderers	1-3	W
29-5-1924	Rotterdam	Sparta Rotterdam-Bolton Wanderers	1-5	W

Tour of 1925

08-5-1925	Wien	Hakoah Wien-Bolton Wanderers	1-2	W
10-5-1925	Budapest	Magyar TK Budapest-Bolton Wanderers	1-1	D
14-5-1925	Wien	First Vienna FC-Bolton Wanderers	2-4	W
17-5-1925	Budapest	Ferencváros TC-Bolton Wanderers	4-1	L
21-5-1925	Praha	Select Praha-Bolton Wanderers	2-0	L

May, 1925 with the Vienna side before a 4–2 win.

Tour of 1928

21-5-1928	Helsingborg	IF Helsingborg-Bolton Wanderers	1-3	W
22-5-1928	Göteborg	IFK Göteborg-Bolton Wanderers	1-3	W
25-5-1928	Göteborg	Örgryte IS-Bolton Wanderers	2-2	D
28-5-1928	Borås	Elfsborg-Bolton Wanderers	0-4	W
30-5-1928	Stockholm	AIK Stockholm-Bolton Wanderers	3-2	L
01-6-1928	Stockholm	Select Stockholm-Bolton Wanderers	1-3	W
03-6-1928	Oslo	Select Oslo-Bolton Wanderers	1-3	W

Tour of 1929

20-5-1929	Barcelona	Select Catalonia-Bolton Wanderers	4-0	L

The 1929 game against a Catalan select side was played as a prelude to the future opening of the new Olympic Stadium and Bolton's Cup successes during this decade is the reason they were invited.

Tour of 1939

14-5-1939	Oslo	Select Norway-Bolton Wanderers	0-4	W
16-5-1939	Fredrikstad	Select Fredrikstad-Bolton Wanderers	1-2	W
18-5-1939	Oslo	Skien Oslo-Bolton Wanderers	1-5	W
21-5-1939	Drammen	Drammen-Bolton Wanderers	0-2	W
23-5-1939	Stavanger	Viking Stavanger-Bolton Wanderers	0-4	W

Note: You will see that even from the early 1900s Bolton were a team of great significance abroad as well as in Britain. The results shown make for impressive reading and the result section for the 1920s enhances the reputation of the teams from that decade as a world class outfit.

INTRODUCTION TO A LEGEND

One cannot encapsulate any history of Bolton Wanderers without the mention of one player in particular. There are many great players who have walked through the gates at Burnden Park and Pikes Lane before that and they are all true legends.

The likes of Joe Smith and David Jack seem to always come to mind first more often than not, but as stated there are many others and hopefully they have all been given passage in this chronicle. However the name Nathaniel Lofthouse is now synonymous with Bolton Wanderers, you cannot mention one without the other. The following chapter of this book is dedicated solely to a truly wonderful player and person.

NATHANIEL 'NAT' LOFTHOUSE: THE MAN–THE LEGEND.

(Our Lofty)

This section of the book is dedicated to the man who seems to have done more individually for Bolton Wanderers than anyone, he is quite simply Bolton Wanderers. After his death on 15 January, 2011 a statue was rightly commissioned and now stands outside the Macron Stadium. There are many reasons why this statue proudly graces the main entrance, some of which are now outlined and are testament to his dedication to the club and football, not just throughout his career but his entire life right to the very end. His last words echo this. "I've got the ball now, it's a bit worn, but I've got it".

He was born on 27 August, 1925 in Bolton and lived in the Tonge Moor area of the town, the youngest of four brothers. His father was a coalbagger then head horse keeper for Bolton Corporation and money was always tight. Regardless of this Lofthouse always said that his parents and brothers backed and encouraged him in every aspect of his footballing journey. Aged ten he went to Castle Hill School, Bolton and was chosen for Bolton and Lancashire school teams. From an early age he was already intellectually aware regarding football history

1943 Bevin Boy

and that his idol the famous Tommy Lawton had attended the same school, he dreamt of emulating his exploits. He once met Lawton at the local bus stop when Lawton was on his way to play for Burnley and he advised Lofthouse that day: 'Always try your best and bang in one or two Nat, its goals that count,' something Lofthouse always remembered. In his first Bolton schools match against Bury he obviously took this quite literally and scored all the goals in a 7–1 win. We must also thank his father's friend, a sportsman called Bert Cole who also knew Tommy Lawton. He had spotted Nat's talent around this time and promised him a bike if he scored a hat-trick against Bury, which duly arrived to Nat's delight. He would take him and his brother Tom training, practicing routines incorporating heading and shooting, which obviously worked! Lofthouse would practise religiously every day, his ambition even then was to be a Bolton player.

He was a fanatical Bolton fan and was overjoyed to be signed by them at the age of just fourteen in 1939, as an amateur. Ironically this was the day after the outbreak of war, all his team heroes had signed up for the forces, so somewhat of an anti-climax as the club had to temporarily close down prior to introduction of the War League. He still had to work though and was a milk boy before working in a local mill and finally as a miner at Mossley Common Colliery, Bolton and it was hard frustrating work, but as Lofthouse said was the best thing that ever happened to him. It hardened him up physically and mentally, turning him into a very fit, strong athlete, which showed in his training and performances for Bolton.

He had signed for a local amateur team called Lomax when Bolton had to close down and he continued to play for them even after he had resumed with Bolton. It was around this time that he was given his chance by Mr Foweraker, which he seized and never looked back, scoring two goals in a 5–1 defeat of Bury in March 1941, age fifteen. It was not long after and inevitable that he was again called in again to see the manager, this time taking his father with him. He was signed on professionally for the handsome fee of £10, a lot of money in those days and Lofthouse said, "I had never seen so much money in my life before". The cheque incidentally was immediately dispatched on his mother's orders into a savings account.

After his Bolton debut he went on to be joint top scorer that season with George Hunt on 14 goals and the rest as they say is now history. He quickly established himself as a crowd favourite especially when Bolton won the two War Cups, North and overall North, South in 1945 and was already firmly established in the team. Bolton also won the Lancashire, Manchester and West Lancashire Cups during his time with the club, along with the two much publicised FA Cup Final appearances in 1953 and 1958. He was Footballer of The Year in 1953 and in 1955–56 was the First Divisions top scorer. In 503 games he scored 285 goals and became the inspirational captain leading the great Bolton sides of the 1950s after Willie Moirs departure. His goal tally does not include goals scored in the war years, which makes him even more remarkable with as previously mentioned over 100 extra goals. He was top scorer in eleven of his official league seasons at Bolton. During his career he did receive a number of serious injuries, as he always threw himself into a game 110 per cent with no half measures, but still managed to recover sufficiently each time to perform at the highest level. After the FA Cup triumph in 1958, Bolton went on a club tour of South Africa and he badly injured his ankle. He recovered sufficiently, but a further knee injury at Birmingham City in 1960 was the end and this time he had to retire as the body was now past recovering sufficiently for top-flight football. He had always pulled in the crowds for Bolton and was much loved by them; in fact he seemed to have had the knack of getting on the right side of any crowd.

Nat is pictured in the Lomax side 1930s front row with trophy at his feet

There is a report from a game in *The Guardian* in 1960, which epitomises him. Lofthouse had recovered from injury in the October and they were to play arch rivals Manchester City in a fiery match at Burnden Park, ironically

Lofthouse with Footballer of the Year award 1953, he was in good company as the previous year it went to Billy Wright and the year following him it was Tom Finney.

on 5 November. The article read: 'a blood and thunder match, no one dared to leave early in case they miss the odd murder or sending off! Bolton knows what it likes however and this is it. The purists rage about the lost arts of English football, but the fact remains that the gate was almost double the average for the season so far, there is a moral here somewhere. Lofthouse was playing inside-right for the first time in ten years that day. At outside-right was a young lad called Francis Lee, aged

1955 before a Bolton match against Chelsea.

sixteen and Lofthouse was tutorial looking after the young lads fortunes, providing encouragement. He was a player who cared deeply for the game and brought the crowd to a heightened state of arousal when Lee took a corner. Lofthouse rose above all and headed the ball into the net, sending over 34,000 fans delirious. To make the day even better the end result was a 3–1 win and the clock was turned back momentarily for the great man. His glory was short lived however as a cheeky Lee announced, "About time with the amount of crosses I've put over". Another news caption read: 'There is English football, there are English footballers. Lofthouse is perhaps the most English of them all.'

He played his first game for England in November, 1950 against Yugoslavia at Highbury. The game ended 2–2 and he scored both the goals. He was not picked again for almost twelve months, which somewhat confused and irritated him. He remarked, "at Bolton though I was getting ahead of myself in terms of ego after the England cap and had a bad game. I was brought soundly back to earth with a sharp word in my ear from George Taylor the

coach, who he respected. He also tells of another ticking off by Taylor when he was told quite frankly, 'that he couldn't trap a bag of washing'. He knew though that he was just keeping his feet firmly on the ground." He went on to play 33 times for his country and scored 30 goals, at that time the record. The game against Austria in Vienna in May, 1952 made him world famous for his heroic and brave display in a 3–2 win scoring two goals including the winner, when he was in plain terms 'taken out' by the Austrian 'keeper. After a short spell off the field with concussion he returned to finish the game but could not remember scoring the third goal. The team and especially Lofthouse received a rousing reception after the final whistle and he was carried from the field as the hero by thousands of soldiers stationed there who had gone to the game, some had gambled their entire wage packets on an England victory. Austria at that time where rated as one of the top, if not the top team in the world and were on paper European Champions. He was then christened the 'Lion of Vienna', a trophy of which was presented to him on his retirement. He also played in three unofficial England games against the USA, Buenos Aires and Rest of Europe. Francis Lee later remarked: "in those days not as many internationals were played, if he was playing today he would have a lot more goals and records."

His Testimonial Programme also gives details of his selection honours by the football league, with whom he was hugely popular. He was

Against Irish League 1952 scoring one of the record six goals for the Football League.

selected on thirteen occasions and scored a further 21 goals and in addition represented the Rest of the UK against Wales in 1951. In one league representative game against the Irish League in 1952 he scored six goals, which is still a record.

After retiring he returned to the club in a coaching capacity in 1967, but in essence had never been away from the place, in fact he was always assisting in any way he could. He was then in unfortunate circumstances handed the managers role when Bill Ridding resigned. He said that he hated the job and did not have that mean streak mentality, "I would lie awake at night worrying about having to tell a player that he was not playing, or if we would win the next match. If we lost I would go straight to bed." He left that position in 1970, though he had to do the role on two other occasions in 1971 and 1985, but only as an interim measure.

He was appointed Club President in 1986 and made a freeman of Bolton in 1989. There was a golden jubilee celebration for him for services to the club in the same year. In 1993 he appeared on *This is Your Life* on ITV and in 1994 awarded an OBE. When the club moved to the Reebok Stadium in 1997 the East Stand was fittingly named after him. He remained in place with the club and always attended right up until ill health prevented him, as he was forever promoting their cause and its charities, totally committed and passionate. On his 80th birthday a party was held at the Reebok in his honour. Gordon Taylor former Bolton player and the President of The Footballers Association began a campaign to get Lofthouse knighted. In 2002 he was an Inaugural Inductee into the English Football Hall of Fame.

Outside the game Nat had married Alma Foster in 1947 and they had known each other since school. They had a son Jeff and daughter Vivien. For a short time they ran the Castle Hotel on Tonge Moor Road,

BOLTON PARISH CHURCH

Funeral Service
and
Service of Thanksgiving for the Life of

Nat Lofthouse OBE

The Lion of Vienna

27th August 1925 - 15th January 2011

Bolton Wanderers and England
Freeman of the Metropolitan Borough of Bolton

26th January 2011

though they believed the environment was unhealthy for the children and moved to the Turton area of Bolton, though tragically Alma died in 1985. He remained there until ailing health in later years meant he had to reside in a local nursing home, where he stayed till his death on 15 January, 2011. His passing was widely reported and publicised, the funeral took place at Bolton Parish Church on 26 January, 2011 and was attended by over 500 including many dignitaries. The streets of the town were packed with people saying goodbye and paying their respects.

Above is the scene at the funeral and the coffin being carried in to the church. In picture left to right carrying are Owen Coyle, Syd Farrimond and Nat's son Jeff. Kevin Davies the then Bolton captain also carried the coffin. After the main funeral a small private family gathering was held at the family's main church, St Anne's in Turton. Nat's memorial stone was laid next to his wife Alma. It was a fitting tribute and send off for Bolton's best ever loved player.

On Wednesday 6 November, 2013 the whole collection of Nat Lofthouse honours and memorabilia was sold off by his family, ironically at the last ever auction held at Bonhams Auctioneers in Chester. Nat's son stated that they wanted the people of Bolton to have access to them as they

Shield presented by the Welsh FA

had no children to pass the collection onto. Bolton Council had already expressed great interest in many of these items, 68 lots in total on the agenda. Because of my obsession with the club and the man himself, I simply had to attend this auction. The idea being simply to be there, see the items first hand and experience the moment because it would never happen again. I have to say the pre- auction viewing and auction itself was quite emotional and I am glad I got the chance to not only see, but hold some of the items he had collected throughout his life.

Every single lot was sold with Bolton Council spending £75,000 in total and included items such as his 1953 and 1958 medals, the ball from the 1958 Final, his shirt from the 1953 Final, plus the Lion of Vienna trophy. They bought fourteen items and the total sale grossed at £102,490.

I lost all sense of reasoning and thought to myself, you have to buy something. In the end I purchased the Trophy presented to him for 20 years loyal service to the Football League and the Shield presented to him after the Rest of UK versus Wales game in 1951, as I already had the programme for that game. I am glad I did it; because I can now say I have on display something which Nat Lofthouse once proudly displayed in his own home and now stands in pride of place in mine. The Football League trophy is seen here on the far left of the photograph as you look at it, with Nat. The photo is from the rear inside cover of his Golden Jubilee souvenir programme of 1989.

I did meet Nat's son Jeff at the auction and had a brief chat with him, a very nice man indeed. He was quite shocked when I asked him to sign my catalogue. "What me?" he asked. "You are the son of my hero and I can't ask him anymore", I replied. He duly signed and I am glad I had that brief conversation, it might not mean much too some people, but it did to me and that's all that matters.

1946 FA Cup semi-final v Charlton.

This is my favourite image of Nat turning out at Burnden. He is in peak condition and a real handful in anyone's books. The modern day version of him was likened to Alan Shearer who was ironically Nat's favourite player after he retired.

With Billy Wright England training 1952, prior to the Italy game.semi-final v Charlton.

England v Rest of World 1953 also billed as Europe. Result a 4–4 draw.

1958 Final action: Nat and Bill Foulkes at toss up before kick- off.

With the FA Cup coming down the Wembley steps.

Bolton Town Hall before the fans, held aloft by Derek Hennin and John Higgins, Bill Ridding is extreme left. Typical Lofthouse in his speech to the people of Bolton he gave thanks to them.

First goal 1958 cup final.

1958 with Alma and FA Cup

I wonder why he was also given the nickname 'Torpedo'! He was renowned for such diving headers. Doug Holden once said he could head the ball as well as he could kick it and he could do that just as well with either foot. He has never seen anyone better.

1959 South Africa tour, Lofthouse introduces the team

This is the man I took to my heart as a child and idolised even though I did not get to know him that well personally, though I feel that I did through my family's stories. He was a totally committed footballer who loved the game, never courted controversy or in any way brought it or his image into disrepute. Time has not in any way tarnished that image, he was the genuine article.

A local lad and one of our own who never tried to be anything else. He knew where he had come from and never forgot it, which is why everyone loved him. We miss him dearly.

Quotes by Lofthouse:

"Football to me is a religion, I live for soccer."

ENGLAND'S
TOP GOAL SCORERS
Nat Lofthouse

HERO-WORSHIP

THE
NAT LOFTHOUSE
TESTIMONIAL
MATCH
BOLTON WANDERERS
1958—CUP FINAL XI
v
INTERNATIONAL ALL STARS XI
1/-

NELSON SQUAR BOLTON.

Left: Nat's former home in Turton and The Castle Hotel (above), which he ran for a short time on Tonge Moor Road, Bolton.

"I was fast, not bad at shooting and could head the ball. I somehow had a knack of being able to get good height and how could anyone fail to score with people like Finney and Matthews crossing the ball for you?"

Quotes about Lofthouse:

"He has a heart as big as a lion, wholehearted commitment. A quality sadly lacking in many great players." **Bobby Charlton**

"He was the perfect centre forward and a leader of the line." Matt Busby.

"In 1966 one person was still talking to us about Nat regarding the Lion of Vienna game 1952, in an effort to inspire us to win the World Cup and that was a certain man called 'Alf Ramsey.'" **Jimmy Greaves.**

"A true lionheart and a great friend. He was feared but also respected." **Tom Finney.**

"A great player and a most likeable man. You always wanted him in your team." **Stan Matthews.**

"A likeable lad always ready to answer the point on the field and could he rise to head the ball. He is a legendary great of English football." **Walter Winterbottom**. England Manager.

"One of the best centre forwards I played with and against." **Billy Wright.**

"He could put thousands on any attendance." **Francis Lee.**

Lion of Vienna pub, Bolton

"I have nothing but the highest regard for Nat Lofthouse." **Harry Gregg.**

"Old fashioned centre-forward who was admired by other countries." **Bobby Robson.**

"England has need of thee at this hour." **Desmond Hackett,** Sports Journalist quote in 1989, he had penned the Lion of Vienna phrase in 1952 after reporting on the game.

"Nat always used to say: 'To kick one Bolton player is like kicking all eleven'." **Roy Hartle**.

"One of the greats of his day and still respected now." **Peter Reid.**

"Nat's achievement is one which is without parallel." **Phil Neal.**

"He is the reason I signed for Bolton as a youth. He is always the hero." **Gordon Taylor.**

Lofthouse Club Honours:

Lancashire Cup runner up 1943–4
War Cup winner (North) 1944–5
War Cup (North/South overall winner) 1944–5
Lancashire Cup winner 1947–8
West Lancashire Cup 1950–1
Manchester Cup runner up 1951–2
Manchester Cup winner 1953–4
FA Cup runner up 1953
FA Cup winner 1958
Charity Shield winner 1958

International Honours: England – 33 games with 30 goals. (three unofficial matches). He broke Vivian Woodward's 47-year-old record when he scored his 30 goals. At this time he was England's top goalscorer.
England B – one game.
Football League Representative Games – 13 with 21 goals. (Still holds record for most goals in one match: six).

OTHER PLAYERS WITH LANCASHIRE CUP WINNING HONOURS

1. James Trainer was born in Wrexham on 7 January, 1863. He initially played for Wrexham then Great Lever in 1883. He signed for Bolton in 1885 and won the Lancashire Cup with them in the same year, when they also secured the Derbyshire and Bolton Charity Cups. He was described as the best goalkeeper in the game and won over 20 caps for Wales. He only has four recorded games for Bolton, though will have played more before his move to Preston North End in 1887 for whom he played over 250 games winning the double with them. After retiring in 1899 he ran The Lamb hotel in Preston before moving to London on business ventures, which failed miserably. He died in abject poverty on 5 August, 1915 aged 52 years.

2. James 'Jimmy' Brogan born 1865 was a forward who began as an amateur at Beith before playing for Hibernians in 1883 scoring six goals on his debut in a 10–1 win. He then had to move to Hearts after complaints about his religious beliefs. He signed for Bolton in 1884 after they had beaten Hearts in a friendly. He won the Charity then Derbyshire Cups with Bolton. He was a winner in two Lancashire Cup finals in 1885–6 and 1891 and was in the side that finished third in 1891–2 in the First Division. He also represented Lancashire select sides. He is recorded with 86 games and 32 goals. On retirement he is believed to have stayed in the area for some time before returned to Scotland as his family had remained there. He is registered with the club till after 1892.

3. Another player from the 1885 Lancashire Cup Final team triumph is **Hough**. He will most probably have participated in the qualifying games to the final against Burnley Wanderers 7–0 in a replay after a 0–0 draw, South Shore 3–1, Blackburn Olympic 11–2, Blackpool St Johns 9–1 and Darwen in the semi-final 2–1.

BOLTON WANDERERS V. EDINBURGH HIBERNIANS.—At Bolton yesterday, a hard contest resulted in a victory for the winners of the Lancashire Cup. M'Ginn scored the first goal for the visitors, but this was soon neutralised by Lundy accidentally heading the ball through his own goal. Hough added a second goal for the Wanderers before half time. After the change of ends Struthers scored twice and Davenport and Hough each once for the Wanderers, while Rose scored for the visitors. Result: Wanderers, six; Hibernians, two.

Hough is in records playing two games with one goal in 1885 in a 6–0 win over Eagley. He is also shown in two friendly games against Hearts and Edinburgh Hibernians in 1886, scoring 2 goals in the second game. The results were on 23 April, 1886 against Hearts 2–2 at Pikes Lane with goals from Struthers and Weir before 8,000 fans, then 26 April, 1886 against Hibs, again at Pikes Lane the score 6–2, other goal scorers were Struthers 2, Davenport and an own goal. Hough was a forward and judging by the amount of goals Bolton scored in the lead up to the Lancashire final will probably have scored others as Bolton had been competing in this competition since 1879. They had beaten Blackburn Rovers in the semi-final the previous year 5–1, but were then expelled for player irregularities, so revenge was sweet. In fact they got the better of Blackburn on many occasions and have a superior win rate over them during this period, this is when Blackburn were regarded as probably the country's best side.

4. Peter Bullough has 52 recorded games from 1888 to 1893 and five goals. He was playing for Bolton pre league and was part of the team that won the Lancashire Cup in 1885–6 and were runners up the following season. His position seems mainly to have been as a centre- or half-back. (Team photo 1889).

5. J. Hewitson was believed to be a local lad and played as a left-winger. Little is known about him in football records. He has three known recorded league games for the club and scored three goals. He obviously

played pre league and scored the only goal in the 1885 Lancashire Cup Final, he is also listed in the team that lost in the Lancashire Final the following season to Preston. There is also a news report for a friendly game against Hibernian scoring one goal in a 3–2 defeat. He then seems to disappear from the scene.

6. Holden another little known of player who graced the 1885 Lancashire Cup Final. He was a defender pre league no other known records. He is most likely in the 1885 team photo.

7. James Parkinson. Was a local player first mentioned after 1883 pre league and also played in the Lancashire Cup Finals in 188556 and 1886–87. He was a full-back who could also play in goal. He is registered with 38 games and one goal and described as a versatile player. He is believed to have been related to the director Peter Parkinson. There was also a D. and W. Parkinson; they may well have been related to him. (See 1889 team photo)

During this time Bolton also secured the services of three Welsh internationals namely **John Powell** a defender, **James Vaughan** a winger and **Bob Roberts** a half-back. They all played for Druids in Wales and moved to Bolton in 1883 and 1884, Roberts being the latter. Powell (1860–1947) was described as a classy defender who could head the ball further than most players could kick it, he was a large presence standing over 6 ft 2in tall, but he and Vaughan only stayed a couple of seasons at Bolton. Powell moved to Newton Heath, later Manchester United and finished his career there. He left Bolton following argument over failing to disclose job commitments to the club leading to investigation by the FA. He was also believed to have been signed by Bolton on professional terms as this had been reported in the Welsh press and professionalism was not legalised until 1885 by which time he had been at Bolton for almost two years. Powell and Vaughan are pictured prior to a Wales game against Scotland in 1880, Vaughan middle row on the left and Powell middle third from left. Powell was capped 15 times and also represented North Wales, Vaughan had four caps. Powell has six recorded games and Vaughan four for Bolton with one goal. (These are pre league statistics.)

8. Robert 'Bob' Roberts was born in July, 1864 and died on 15 March, 1932. He came to Bolton in 1888 and re-joined his teammates from Druids, Powell and Vaughan. He is registered with 85 games and five goals for Bolton though as with other players he also played pre league games and cup matches, so probably had more. He was a runner up in the 1885–86 Lancashire Cup and a winner in 1890–91. He transferred to Preston North End in 1892 and finished his career at Lincoln City. He played nine times for Wales with one goal. He was described as a tough looking player and was also a very good boxer. He was a good sprinter recorded at 13 seconds over 120 yards. A newspaper report of the time described him as the best half-back in English football with superb ball skills. On retirement he lived in an Alms house in Ruabon, Wales, which had all the walls covered in reports for Bolton, Preston and Wales. He was known locally as 'Bob Bolton'. (See Bolton team photo 1889)

Roberts is back right in the Preston team photo next to Jimmy Trainer.

9. James Munro. Born 1870 in Dundee and played locally before signing for Bolton in 1890. He played 52 games for the club and scored 21 goals. He was in the side that won the Lancashire Cup in 1891 and the team that finished third the following year scoring 12 goals. He

was a multi task player and could play just about any position equally well, even in goal. He moved to Burton Swifts the following year then to Swindon Town, where he became club captain and was idolised there. He also won Southern League representative honours. The local paper described him as 'lion hearted'.

An 'In Memoriam' card from the time gave the following words:

A star from out our ranks has gone,
A light which shone the best,
No more he'll play the manly game,
For Jimmy has gone to rest.

Gone from us, but not forgotten,
Never shall thy memory fade,
Sweetest thoughts shall ever linger,
Round the spot where thou art laid.

In 1898 after playing in a 4–3 win over Tottenham on New Year's Eve, he fell ill and it was thought he had a bad cold. His condition deteriorated and he died just four days later on 4 January, 1899 aged 28 years. He left a wife and five-month-old daughter. The cause of death was spinal meningitis.

10. John 'Jack' McNee was born in Renton, Dunbartonshire in 1867. He played for Renton Wanderers before signing for Renton FC around 1887–88 as an inside-forward. They were then regarded as a top class side. He won the Glasgow and Scottish Cup with them, scoring in the 1888 Scottish Final in a 6–1 win against Cambuslang FC. He moved to Bolton in 1889 and scored the only Bolton goal in a 2–1 FA Cup semi-final defeat against Sheffield United. He then won the Lancashire Cup with Bolton in 1890–91.

He played 96 games for Bolton with 25 goals before moving to Newcastle United in 1894. His other clubs were West Hereford later Watford, winning the Southern League with them in 1900, before ending his career at Fulham.

11. Tom Barber was born on 22 July, 1886 and died on 18 September, 1925. He was born in Newcastle under the shadow of St James' Park, playing locally before signing for Bolton in 1908. He played 107 games and scored 14 goals playing as either a half-back or inside-forward. He

played in the Lancashire Cup final in 1911–12 scoring a goal in the 4–1 win over Burnley. He was sold to Aston Villa in 1912 for £1,950 and the fee paid for the Great Lever stand at Burnden.

He scored the only goal for them in the 1913 FA Cup Final against Sunderland. He fought in the first war and was wounded, but recovered to guest for a number of clubs including Celtic and also represented the Footballers Battalion. He ended his career at Walsall, but died aged 39 years from tuberculosis.

12. Alfred 'Alf' Bentley was born on 15 September, 1887 in Alfreton and died on 15 April, 1940 in his home town aged 52. He was a centre-forward and initially played for Derby County from 1906 before signing for Bolton in 1911 for £1,000. He had top scored for Derby in season 1908–09 with 24 goals in the Second Division, with eight more in FA Cup matches. He played 55 games for Bolton and scored 16 recorded goals. He scored two in the Lancashire final of 1911–12. In 1913 he moved the West Brom and scored four goals on his debut against Burnley. He won the First Division with them in 1919–20 and the Charity Shield to secure his place in Baggies folklore. (Front row third from left).

13. James Fay was born in Southport on 29 March, 1884 and died in 1957 in Southport. He played locally then at Chorley and Oldham Athletic in 1907, before signing for Bolton in 1911 as a centre-half. During the war he was registered with Southport and guested for Bolton and Preston. He then returned to Bolton in 1919 and represented the Football League in the same year against the Scottish League. He played 136 games and scored five goals at one stage captaining the club. He won the Lancashire Cup with Bolton in 1911–12. He was also with Bolton when they won the Manchester Cup in 1920–21.

He finished his career back at Southport joining them in 1921 and was secretary of the Players Association until 1952 and a founder member of the Players Union. He ran a sport's outfitters in Southport, later becoming a Justice of the Peace; he had the nickname 'Gentleman James.'

14. Jack Feebury was born in Hucknall on 10 May, 1888 and died in Nottingham in 1960. He joined Bolton in 1908, a full-back who could kick equally well with either foot. His brother was also registered with the club. Jack played 192 games and scored 16 goals. He replaced local boy **Jack Slater** who was to leave the game and become a prominent businessman and MP. Mr Slater became a multi-millionaire as a coal merchant, then a major industrialist.

Feebury won a Lancashire Cup medal in 1911 and was with the club when they won the Manchester Cup in 1908–09. In 1920 he transferred to Exeter City where he played with Dick Pym, before ending his career at Brighton and Mid-Rhondda United. During the war he guested for a number of clubs including Notts County and Southampton.

15. Harold Hilton was born on 13 November, 1889 in Bebbington and died on 9 December, 1971. He played for Tranmere Rovers when he

was only seventeen and Bolton signed him in 1910 as an inside-forward for £2.10 shillings a week, a tidy sum in those days. Tranmere complained but it was pointed out he was a free agent and the decision stood. He worked for Levers at Port Sunlight until signing for Bolton. He played 65 games and scored 24 goals for the club, playing in the Lancashire Cup Final in 1911. During the war he guested for Tranmere and returned there from Bolton in 1920 where he finished his career, becoming player manager for one season in 1923. His son also called Harold spent a brief spell at Bolton in 1931, but he could not break through into the first team. Harold is pictured above left and in the 1910 team photo with Whiteside.

16. Ernest 'Ernie' Whiteside pictured left was born in Lytham and joined Bolton from there in 1908 as a half-back. He played 88 games for Bolton including the Lancashire Cup Final of 1911 and was with the club when they won the Manchester Cup in 1908–09. He was eventually displaced by Walter Rowley and moved to York City in 1914. On retirement he had a newspaper business in Bolton before moving to Anglesey in North Wales.

17. Sydney Newton was born in Tyldesley circa 1890 and played for Bolton between 1910 and 1912, with 15 recorded games as a 'keeper. He is then registered at Preston North End in 1914 and little is known of him after the outbreak of the war, as he is not in player records. He won the Lancashire Cup with Bolton in 1911–12. He is believed to have died in 1944.

18. Jack Atkinson was born in New Washington, Tyne and Wear on 20 December, 1913. He played for the Washington Colliery before signing for Bolton in 1931. He was a centre-half described as, of tremendous stature. He was the main stay of the team the defence being built around him.

He played 263 games for Bolton and scored five goals. He reached the semi-final of the FA Cup in 1935 with Bolton when they were also promoted from the Second Division in the same year. He won the Lancashire Cup with Bolton in 1933–34, 1938–39 and the Manchester Cup 1937–38. His career was affected by the war and as previously stated he served with the Police and then the 53rd Field Regiment in Italy. He played for Bolton till 1939 later guesting for Bolton, Everton and Blackpool during the conflict. After the war he was restricted to limited appearances until 1947–48 when he took over as player manager of New Brighton. On retirement he was a licensee in Bolton. He died in 1977.

19. John 'Jack' Bradley was born 27 November, 1916 in Hemsworth, Yorkshire and died on 14 December, 2002. He played for a number of clubs before Bolton namely Huddersfield, Swindon Town and Chelsea. He signed for Bolton in 1947–48 and played 99 games scoring 20 goals. He was an inside-forward and regarded as a real tough character. During the war he was in the Police War Reserve, then the RAF in 1940. He served with them all over England and guested for several clubs.

He was well-thought-of at Bolton and Nat Lofthouse later quoted: "By God! Jack Bradley, he had the best left foot I have ever seen in my life." Bradley won the Lancashire Cup with Bolton in 1947–8, scoring one of the goals in a 5–1 defeat of Southport at Haig Avenue.

In 1950 he transferred to Norwich City then managed Great Yarmouth. On retirement he managed the Jolly Farmer pub in the area. His father had been a professional footballer, as was his uncle who won the First Division Championship with Liverpool in 1905–06.

Bradley is second from left, back row in the 1948 team photo.

As a matter of interest front row second from right is Harry McShane who later played for Manchester United. He is the father of Ian McShane the actor, probably best known for playing the character Lovejoy in the series of the same name.

20. Ralph Banks is detailed in the section after the 1953 FA Cup Final. In addition to the Cup Final he won the Lancashire Cup with Bolton in 1947–48 and the Richardson Cup in 1950–51 and as stated was brother of Tommy Banks, they are pictured together.

21. Thomas Cullen Duckworth was born in Tonge, Bolton on 2 October, 1908. He played locally for Darwen then Blackpool. He signed for Bolton in 1931 and played 29 recorded games. He won a Lancashire Cup winner medal in 1931–32. In 1933 ex Wanderer Ted Vizard the manager of Swindon Town signed him and he played over 137 games for them. In 1937 he transferred to Darwen, then Southport and finally Horwich RMI.

Duckworth is back row second from left. Ted Vizard is middle centre in the suit.

22. George Richard Eastham was born on 13 September, 1914 in Blackpool and died in 2000 in South Africa. He played locally for South Shore and signed for Bolton in 1932, playing 131 games and scored 17 goals as an inside-forward. In 1933–34 he secured a Lancashire Cup

Pictured above, George his brother Harry and George Eastham junior.

winners medal at Maine Road in a 4–2 win against Oldham Athletic, scoring one of the goals in the Final. He helped Bolton reach the FA Cup semi-final in 1934–35 when they were also promoted back to the First Division in second place behind Brentford. His form was so good at this stage he won an England cap against Holland in 1935 and one appearance for the League team with two goals. Bolton then struggled for a while in the First Division and he was sold to Brentford in 1935–36 for £4,500. He did play for a number of clubs after this and finished his career at Ards in Ireland who he player managed from 1953–58. He then managed a number of other Irish clubs and Accrington Stanley before retiring in 1974.

He had joined the forces during the war and guested for numerous clubs including Bolton. His brother Harry played for Liverpool and he also guested for Bolton during the war. George's son also George was a footballer of high repute and he played for a number of clubs including Arsenal and Stoke City, who he also managed. He won 19 England caps with two goals.

In tribute:

23. Henry 'Harry' Goslin was born in Willington, County Durham on 9 November, 1909 and died in Italy on 18 December, 1943 from wounds sustained in combat. He was signed by Bolton from Boots Athletic in 1930 for £25 as a replacement for Fred Kean. He was a central-defender

of immense stature and became team captain in 1936, was well settled in the area and ran a cycle shop in the town. He was a leading figure and talisman for the team who everyone respected and he was a true gentleman. He played 334 games and scored 23 goals. He won the Lancashire Cup with Bolton in 1933–34 and 1938–39. Bolton also won the Manchester Cup in 1937–38 and reached the FA Cup semi-final in 1934–35.

He is forever remembered for giving the emotive speech at Burnden Park on 8 April, 1939 before a game against Sunderland. From the centre circle by microphone he stated everyone had a duty to help in the impending conflict with Germany. A game which incidentally they then won 2–1. The whole team signed up after the game for the 53rd Field Regiment, Lancashire Artillery.

He guested for Bolton, Chelsea and Norwich during the war when he was available. He also gained selection to the England wartime team and the British Army (three games). He was well thought of in the forces and rose to the rank of Lieutenant through his actions and leadership.

He was mortally wounded on 14 December in battle near the River Sangro between Taranto and Foggia, Italy by shrapnel from mortar fire and died four days later. He is buried in the Sangro River war cemetery. He left a wife and two children behind who were given great support by the club, with a £650 benefit going to his widow. One of Harry's sons Bob became a respected senior figure with Bolton Police, then in Yorkshire and Cambridgeshire.

24. Albert Geldard was born on 11 April, 1914 in Bradford and died on 8 October, 1989. He made his debut aged just fifteen for Bradford Park Avenue in 1928 as a winger. He was signed by Everton in 1932 and played over 180 games for them. Bolton signed him in 1938 for £4,500. Tommy Lawton expressed his dismay at letting him go stating: "He is the fastest thing I've seen over 10 yards on two legs". He was described as a wing wizard with exceptional speed, could shoot well with both feet and was a great goal provider. He won the FA Cup with Everton in 1933 and the Lancashire Cup in 1934–35 scoring two goals in a 3–1 win against Bury.

He is pictured and with the 1938–39 Bolton team picked for the tour of Norway, front third from left. He assisted Bolton in reaching the FA Cup semi-finals in 1945–46 as a guesting player.

He used to travel from Liverpool with Stan Hanson to Burnden, he knew Stan through his brother Alf Hanson who played for Liverpool, and he had become friends with him when playing in the Merseyside derbies. He only played 39 games for the club as he joined up for the war with the other Bolton players and this in effect finished his career, playing one more season when hostilities ceased. He played semi-professionally for Darwen, but a knee injury finished his career in 1947. He represented England on four occasions between 1933 and 1937. He won a Lancashire Cup medal with Bolton in 1938–39.

He is pictured and with the 1938–39 Bolton team picked for the tour of Norway, front third from left. He assisted Bolton in reaching the FA Cup semi-finals in 1945–46 as a guesting player.

25. Thomas Percival Griffiths was born in Wrexham on 21 February, 1906 and died on 25 December, 1981. He began his career at Wrexham as a centre-half then Everton, signing for Bolton in 1931 playing 53 games with eight goals. He won the Lancashire Cup with Bolton in 1931–32. He then transferred to Middlesbrough and later played for Aston Villa, before ending his career back at Wrexham. Between 1927 and 1937 he played for Wales 21 times with three goals.

26. Matthew Muirhead 'Matt' Gillies was born in Loganlea, Scotland on 12 August, 1921 and died on 24 December, 1998. He played locally and for RAF Weeton during the war and was a defender. He was officially signed by Bolton in 1946 after guesting during the latter war years, staying till 1952. He played 154 games and scored one goal. He won the Lancashire Cup with Bolton in 1947–48 and was at the club when they won the West Lancashire Cup in 1950–51. He moved to Leicester City in 1952, winning the Second Division in 1953–54. After 1956 he eventually became their manager staying till 1968. He won the League Cup in 1964 and was runner up in 1963. He also guided them to two losing FA Cup Finals in 1961 and 1963. He moved to Nottingham Forest in 1969 before retiring in 1972. Before leaving Forest he signed John Robertson and Martin O'Neill who won the European Cup there under Brian Clough. He was renowned for his technical abilities as a manager and was highly thought of by both Matt Busby and Bill Shankly.

27. Harold Howarth was born on 25 November, 1908 in Little Hulton and died in 1974. He had played football locally and signed for Bolton in 1929, he played 61 recorded games. As previously stated his father had played for Bolton. He won the Lancashire Cup in 1931–32 and was with the club when Bolton won the West Lancashire Cup and the Richardson Cup in 1930–31. He then transferred to Chester City in 1934–35 playing over 178 games for them with seven goals prior to the war. He ended his career at Southport in 1945.

28. George John 'Jack' Hurst was born on 27 October, 1914 at Lever Bridge, Bolton. He joined the club in 1934 and played 73 games with two goals, helping Bolton win promotion back into the First Division and they also reached the FA Cup semi-final in 1935. He won a Lancashire Cup winners medal in 1938–39 then signed up for the war effort in 1939, though he did guest for the club when available. He was at Bolton when they won the Manchester Cup in 1937–38 He was part of the squad that reached the FA Cup semi-final in 1945–46 and moved to Oldham Athletic in 1947 playing for them for four years. He then had one season at Chelmsford City before retiring.

29. Don Howe was born in Wakefield on 26 November, 1917 and died in 1978. He signed for Bolton in 1933 and stayed his whole career, which was interrupted by the war when he signed up with the rest of the side. He made his debut in 1936 as a winger but was capable of playing in almost any position. He was part of the famous 53rd regiment and was one of many evacuated from Dunkirk along with other team members in the same regiment. He was wounded in 1943 but returned to army duties seeing out the end of the war, reaching the rank of Battery Sergeant Major during the conflict. He played for the Army and guested for Bolton, Norwich and Newcastle.

After 1945 he became club captain as Harry Goslin had unfortunately been killed. He played 286 games and scored 35 goals. He won the Lancashire Cup with Bolton in 1947–48. He was also part of the squad that won the same competition in 1938–39, the Manchester Cup in 1937–38 and the West Lancashire Cup in 1950–51. He played in the team that reached the FA Cup semi-final in 1945–46. He was a qualified FA coach but eventually retired to work for a paper merchant in the area after 1952.

30. James 'Jimmy' Jackson was born in Glasgow on 1 January, 1921 and played locally. He came to Bolton in 1947 as an inside-forward after the war and had guested in 1941–42, reports state: 'he was a fast pacey player with good skills.' He is only listed with 11 games and one goal. He did play in the Lancashire Cup final 1947–48 in the win over Southport. In 1950 he transferred to Carlisle United when Bill Shankly signed him. He played over 100 games for them and was a highly rated player. He is listed in their all-time top 100 players list. He is believed to have retired around 1954.

31. Edwin 'Eddie' Morris Jones was born on 20 April, 1914 in Abercynon, Wales and died in 1984. He is only registered with one league game for Bolton with one goal in 1933, he was a winger. He played in the Lancashire Cup Final of 1933–34 in a 4–2 victory against Oldham Athletic. He is more than likely to have played more than one game in other similar competitions and friendlies, but these statistics are not readily available.

He is then registered in 1936 at Swindon Town making 189 appearances for them with 34 goals, again under ex Wanderer Ted Vizard. His football was affected by the war and he is last recorded at Swindon in 1946–7 before finishing his career at Chippenham Town. He also represented Wales at junior level.

32. Robert 'Bob' Jones was born in Everton on 9 January, 1902 and died in 1989. He played initially for Everton then Southport and was signed by Bolton in in 1929 as a 'keeper because Dick Pym was nearing the end of his career with the club. He played 244 games for Bolton and won the Lancashire Cup in 1933–34. Bolton was promoted from the Second Division in 1935, when they also reached the FA Cup semi-final. They won the West Lancashire Cup when he was there in 1930–31. He moved to Cardiff City in 1937 and stayed there till late 1939. He was about to retire, but Southport persuaded him to return and he played for them again before being appointed trainer in 1947, meeting Bolton in the Lancashire Final. He continued playing till after 1950 with the reserves, he was then aged 48. He retired in the 1970s and moved to Great Harwood to support his son also called Bob who was a goalkeeper. He continued to work and assist there till he was 85 years of age. His health then deteriorated and he later died of pneumonia. He is still held in high regard at Southport and Harwood as a footballing legend and great servant to the game.

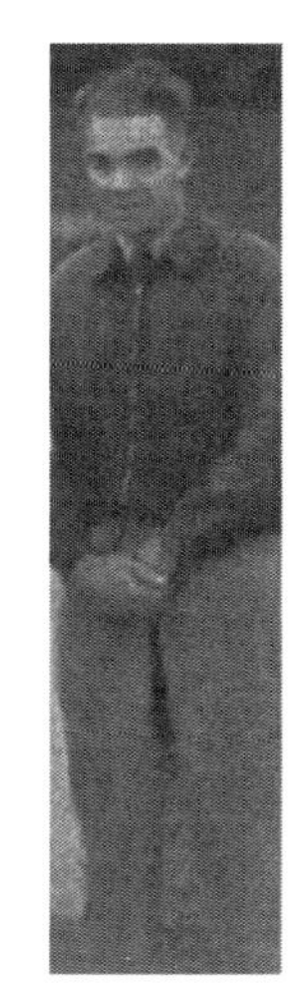

33. Jack Milsom was born on 22 February, 1907 in Bedminster and died in 1977. He played locally then signed for Bristol Rovers followed by Kettering then Rochdale. He signed for Bolton in 1929 and replaced Harold Blackmore, Bolton paying £1,750 for his services. He was a centre-forward and prolific goalscorer, being top scorer at Bolton from 1932 to 1937. He had broken his leg in 1930 so it was around 1932 before he was the regular first choice. In 1932–33 Bolton was relegated, but gained promotion back to the First Division in 1935, with Milson remaining in good form.

He played 255 games and scored 153 goals. He then transferred to Manchester City in 1938 for £4,000, but retired in 1940. He won the Lancashire Cup with Bolton in 1931–32.

34. John 'Jackie' Roberts was born in Swansea on 30 May, 1918 and died in June, 2001. He played junior football for Cwmburia and Wales Schoolboys, he also won one full international cap in 1949. He joined Bolton in 1936 and was an inside-forward, but could play in other positions. His career was interrupted by the war and he also joined the 53rd field regiment. He represented the armed forces and also guested for Swansea and Norwich City. He was wounded in Italy in 1944 and returned home, recovering to play for Bolton in the Football League North games. In 1950 he transferred to Swansea for £5,000, but was troubled by knee injuries and finished his career at Llanelli. On retirement he then worked at the steel works in Swansea. He played 171 games for Bolton and scored 19 goals. He won the Lancashire Cup with Bolton in 1947–48. Bolton also won the West Lancashire Cup during his time with the club.

35. Edward 'Teddy' Rothwell was born in Atherton on 3 September, 1917 and died in 2000. He signed in 1937–38 from local football as a winger and played in the Lancashire Cup Final in 1938–39. His career was greatly affected by the war and although he was at Bolton until season 1948–49 he only played 48 games with two goals, though he did guest during the War League years. He moved to Southport in 1949 and spent two seasons there before retiring from football.

36. Thomas Mc Kenzie Sinclair was born on 13 October, 1921 in Shettleston near Glasgow. He signed for Bolton in 1938–39 playing 10 games with five goals, he was a winger. He then signed up with his teammates for the war and played a handful of games near the end of

the war. He was in the team that won the Lancashire Cup in 1939. He guested for Leicester City during the war and played in the army team with other Bolton players. He attained the rank of Sergeant.

In 1946 he is registered playing for Gainsborough then Aldershot till 1950, he also played for Brentford and Bradford City. He is pictured left.

37. Robert 'Bob' Smith was born on 15 December, 1912 in Atherton and played for Bolton between 1932 and 1936 playing 102 games. He was a full-back and played in the Lancashire Cup winning side of 1933–34 and reached the semi-final of the FA Cup in 1935. After being injured he was moved on to Colwyn Bay then Huddersfield Town in 1936, though he could not hold a first team place as injuries had taken their toll. He retired in 1937. (Pictured left.)

38. George Thomas Taylor was born on 12 December, 1907 in Walsall. He played locally and achieved England schoolboy honours. He signed for Notts County in 1925 playing 265 games with 46 goals for them before moving to Bolton in 1933 for £3,500. He was a winger of great skill and was part of the Bolton side winning promotion back to the First Division in 1935 and reaching the FA Cup semi-final in the same year. He played 170 games for the club and scored 29 goals. He won a Lancashire Cup winners medal in 1933–34 and was with Bolton when they won the Manchester Cup in 1937–38. He transferred to Coventry City in the same season. During the war he guested for Leicester City.

39. Raymond William 'Ray' Westwood was born in Brierley Hill, Kingswinsford, West Midlands on 14 April, 1912 and died in January,

1982. He signed in 1928 when former Bolton defender Jack Round recommended him. He made his debut in 1931 and was a striker of prolific speed and skill. He was the David Beckham type of his day and a number of companies used him for advertising purposes, such as Brylcreem. He was a favourite of the young Nat Lofthouse, so he must have been good. He was also the uncle of Manchester United legend Duncan Edwards.

He played 333 games and scored 144 goals. His career was again controlled by the war and he signed up with the other players for the 53rd regiment, but was unhappy throughout the whole campaign. He just wanted to play football and Army football did not satisfy his desire. In 1947 he moved to Chester City then ended his career at Darwen. On retirement he had a newsagents shop in his home town.

Pre match watched by Milsom and Atkinson

He won the Lancashire Cup with Bolton in 1931–32, 193–34 and 1938–39. Bolton also won the West Lancashire Cup and Richardson Cup in 1930–31. He reached the FA Cup semi-final with Bolton in 1934–35 and 1945–46. He won promotion back to the First Division with Bolton in 1934–45.

Westwood won six England caps and but for the war would have been a lot more, he was an exceptionally talented player. He also represented the Football League on six occasions.

40. Danny Winter was born in Tonypandy, Wales on 14 June, 1918 and died on 22 March, 2004 in Trealaw, Wales. He joined Bolton in 1936 as a full-back and is registered with them up to 1939, when with the outbreak of the war he signed up for the 53rd field regiment. He guested for Chelsea during the war and in the 1944–5 War Cup, but did not play against Bolton in the Final, as he was still on the books. He transferred to Chelsea for £5,000 in 1945 after playing for the Wales War Team and in the Army side during the conflicts. He had played 37 games for Bolton and won a Lancashire Cup medal in 1939. He made a number of guest appearances for Bolton during the war. A serious ankle injury in 1950 ended his career.

OTHER PLAYERS WITH LANCASHIRE CUP RUNNERS-UP MEDALS

1. Thomas Henry Barlow was born in Bolton in 1873 he was an inside -orward who played initially for Halliwell Rovers before signing for Bolton in 1898 playing 90 games with 25 goals before he left in 1904. He did however spend a year with Southampton from 1902 as Jack Picken became first choice. He was allowed back the next season, as he was homesick. He had played in the Lancashire Cup Final in 1898–99.

In 1904 he transferred to Millwall before returning to the area again the following year to play for Atherton, then finished his career at Oldham Athletic in the Lancashire Combination where they finished as Champions, helping them to election into the Football League.

2. Robert 'Bob' Brown was born in Cambuslang, Scotland in 1870. He began his football career locally at Blantyre Thistle before signing for Sheffield Wednesday in 1892–93. He was a versatile player who could play in just about any position and did so for Bolton barring the 'keeper's role. After a spell at Third Lanark in 1895 he joined the Wanderers and stayed at the club until 1901–02, though was briefly loaned out to Burnley. He played 136 games with 14 goals and played in the first ever league game at Burnden Park. He played in the Lancashire Cup Final of 1898–99.

He retired in 1903 and worked in the Insurance business.

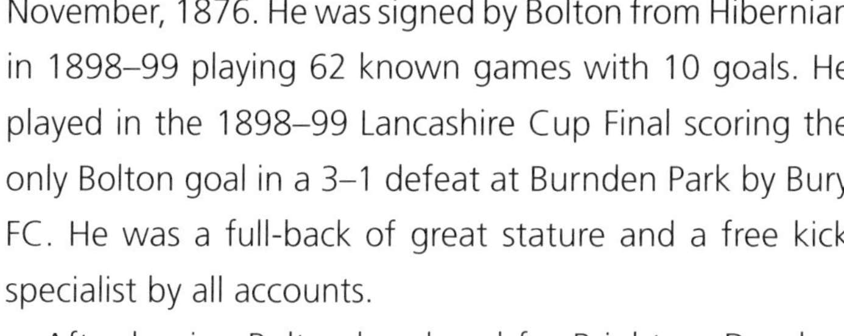

3. Thomas McAteer was born in Glasgow on 18 November, 1876. He was signed by Bolton from Hibernian in 1898–99 playing 62 known games with 10 goals. He played in the 1898–99 Lancashire Cup Final scoring the only Bolton goal in a 3–1 defeat at Burnden Park by Bury FC. He was a full-back of great stature and a free kick specialist by all accounts.

After leaving Bolton he played for Brighton, Dundee, Carlisle and Clyde, he then signed for Celtic in 1910, winning a Scottish Cup winners medal in 1911 in a 2–0 win against Hamilton scoring one of the goals, with what was described as a screamer of a shot. He retired in 1912 for a short while then began playing again for Albion Rovers prior to the war. He was then injured in action, which forced his full retirement and he returned to work in the pits, where he had started prior to his football career. He died on 20 September, 1959 aged 83 years.

4. Robert 'Bob' Jack was born on 4 April, 1876 in Alloa, Scotland and began his career with them in 1891 till 1895. He moved to Bolton in 1895 playing 125 games scoring 29 goals, top scoring for the club in 1897 and was part of the promotion side in 1900. He played in the Lancashire Cup Final in 1898–99 against Bury. He then moved to Preston North End in 1901. His other clubs were Glossop, Port Vale and then Plymouth as both player and manager where he was revered. He then moved to Southend United in 1906 performing a similar role winning the Southern League Division Two title. He returned to manage Plymouth in 1910 staying till 1938, winning the Southern title again and entry into the Football League. Plymouth won the Third Division title in 1929.

His more famous son is David Jack who was the footballing legend with Bolton, Arsenal and England. His other sons Rollo and Donald Jack also played for Bolton. Robert died on 6 May, 1943 aged 67 years and his ashes were scattered over the Plymouth Argyle pitch at Home Park.

5. Hugh Morgan was born in Lanarkshire in 1875/6 and began his career at Harthill Thistle before signing for Airdrie. He moved to Sunderland in at the end of 1896. Bolton then signed him in 1898 for £200 as a forward and he went on to play 47 registered games scoring 16 goals. He played in the losing Lancashire Final of 1898–89. He moved to Newton Heath in 1901, then in the same year to Manchester City. His other clubs included Accrington Stanley and Blackpool, where he finished his career.

6. David Willocks was from the Dundee area and came to Bolton in season 1892–93, staying until the end of 1893–94 season. He played as an inside-forward playing 36 registered games with eight goals. He then moved to Burton Swifts followed by Dundee FC, where he was a regular scorer for both clubs. He is still listed in 1898–99 on the score sheet in games for Dundee FC. His final club is believed to have been Brighton United after this date. The sketch below is from an ad for the 1894 FA Cup Final, although he did not play in this due to injury.

He played in the Lancashire Cup final in 1893–94 when Bolton were beaten 2–1 by Everton at Hyde Road, Manchester.

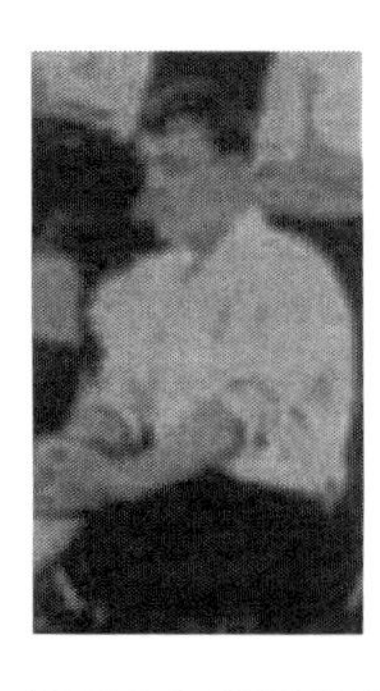

7. George Ferguson was an inside-forward who could also play at centre-half. He was at Bolton from 1893–94 until 1895–96 and he is registered with 19 games and three goals. He played in the Lancashire Cup Final in 1893–94 and scored Bolton's only goal in the defeat by Everton. No other details are registered for him in records.

8. Albert Gilligan was an inside forward who played 107 games for the club with 17 goals, registered on Boltons books from 1893-4 till 1899-1900. During his time at Bolton he did spend time on loan to Dundee FC. He played in the Lancashire Cup final in 1898-9.

9. George Lockhart was born in 1877 in Barhill, Scotland. He is registered with Bolton from 1897-1900 playing 28 games as a left back. He then moved on to Burnley FC. He also played in the 1898-9 Lancashire Cup final for Bolton and little is known of him after 1902.

OTHER EARLY BOLTON PLAYERS WITH REPRESENTATIVE HONOURS DURING THEIR CAREER

W. BANNISTER.
Burnley F.C. and Bolton Wanderers F.C.

William 'Bill' Bannister was born in 1879 in Burnley and died on 25 March, 1942 aged 53. He signed for Bolton from Burnley in 1901 as a centre-back and played 30 games with three goals for the club before he left in 1903. He represented England on two occasions and had one appearance for the League representative side.

His other clubs were Woolwich Arsenal, Leicester Fosse and finally back to Burnley. On retirement he was a licensee in the Leicester area.

John 'Jack' Fitchett was born in 1879 in Chorlton-cum-Hardy. He joined Bolton in 1897–98 season as a full back and played 81 games with four goals. He also played for Manchester United, Southampton, Manchester City, Fulham, Plymouth Argyle, Sale and Exeter City. He did retire at one stage as he was an actor and member of the Fred Carno Company, appearing at one time with Charlie Chaplin. He played for Bolton in the losing 1898–99 Lancashire Cup Final and played two league representative matches with two goals. He had an unofficial representative

appearance for England against Germany in 1901, the result 10–1 in England's favour. He managed Plymouth for a short time replacing the former Bolton manager Frank Brettell.

On retirement he became a theatrical manager and was also the licensee of The Royal Sovereign in Plymouth. This last information on him was from around 1938. He is pictured below.

David Weir was born in 1863 in Aldershot. He moved to Scotland with his family as a child and initially played his football there. He was playing for Maybole, south of Glasgow before joining Halliwell in 1887 and scored all eight goals for them in a match against Notts County. He was listed as a half-back and joined Bolton the following year, though he had tenacity for scoring goals. He registered the clubs first hat-trick in 1888 against Accrington Stanley and also scored four in the record 13–0 demolition of Sheffield United in the FA Cup in 1890. He moved to Ardwick, later Manchester City in the same year winning two Manchester Cups with them, though he returned in 1893. He was a player of temperament and this caused his omission from the FA Cup Final side in 1894, due to his disagreements with other team members. In 92 games for the club he scored 41 goals and was undoubtedly a player of quality. He played in two losing Lancashire Cup Finals in 1892–93 and 1893–94. He won two England caps, with two goals. In 1895 he returned to Maybole. On retirement he managed Glossop North End and then coached in Stuttgart from 1911. He died in Bolton in 1933, the report on 8 December states he became ill after catching a chill watching a Bolton game and never recovered.

Albert Shepherd was born on 10 September, 1885 in Great Lever, Bolton and died in Bolton on 8 November, 1929. He played locally and signed initially for Blackburn before moving to Bolton in 1904. He became

a very strong tough player and prolific goalscorer with a ferocious shot and in 123 games scored 90 goals. He was with Bolton when they won the Manchester Cup in 1905–06 and also represented the league side on one occasion. He fell out of favour with the fans when he chose to move to Newcastle United in 1908. His move to them paid off, as he became a legend there winning the First Division and FA Cup in 1909 and 1910 and was the division's top scorer on a number of occasions. He was the first Newcastle player to score more than 30 goals in a season. He played 123 games and scored 92 goals for them. He strangely only won one England cap with one goal, though he did get called up for the First World War. He later played for Bradford City before retiring.

He then took charge of the Crown and Cushion on Mealhouse Lane, Bolton, which is one of the oldest pubs in Bolton, though the original building was demolished in 1900. Incidentally another former Bolton player Bethel Robinson had also managed the pub and is famed for playing in the first ever league game for Bolton against Derby County. Albert Shepherd died on these premises in 1929. He was 44 years of age.

Robert 'Bob' Glendenning was born in Washington, Durham on 6 June, 1888 and died on 19 November, 1940, he is buried in Bolton. He initially played for Barnsley from 1908 as a half-back appearing in two FA Cup Finals, 1910 against Newcastle and 1912, playing on the winning side against West Brom. Both Finals went into extra-time and he set up the winning goal in the 1912 Final in the last minute of the extra-time period. He moved to Bolton in 1912–13 and stayed till 1914–15 playing 83 games, Bolton also reached the FA Cup semi-final and the Final of the Manchester Cup before the intervention of the war and his departure. During the war he guested for Burnley and after 1918 ended his career at Accrington Stanley. He played in an unofficial match for England against Scotland in 1914; the result was 2–0 in England's favour.

He then coached in Holland and became manager of the national side and Koninklijke FC, holding both roles. He managed the national side for the 1928 Olympics and two World Cups 1934 and 1938 ending his time with them in 1940, again because of the intervention of war. He died later the same year. He still holds the record of most victories for a Holland team manager and is highly thought of and remembered by them and the Koninklijke club (KNVB) to this day, who maintain his headstone. He is pictured in 1940 with the national side.

Alexander 'Alex' Pollock Donaldson was born in Barrhead, Scotland on 4 December, 1890. He played for local teams in the Yorkshire/Midlands area before briefly joining Sheffield United on trial around 1912. He signed for Bolton in that year from Ripley Athletic for £50. He was a winger of good skill and was almost chosen to play for England in a trial match in 1914, until his birthplace was realised. He did however play six times for Scotland between 1914 and 1922, with a further three unofficial games only appearing on the losing side once; he had one goal to his name and won the home internationals with Scotland in 1922. He played 146 games for Bolton with six goals, but the war and injuries seriously affected his career though Bolton did win the Manchester Cup in 1920–21 during his time with them. He worked in munitions during the war and guested for Leicester City playing 51 games with six goals. In 1921 he transferred briefly to Sunderland then Manchester City, before ending his career at Ashton National then Chorley.

ALEC. DONALDSON

On retirement he had a sports shop in Gorton, before becoming licensee of the Gardeners Arms in Bolton. He died in 1972.

Evan Jones was born on 20 October, 1888 in Treharfod, Wales and died in 1972. He initially played for his home town then Aberdare Athletic before signing for Chelsea in 1909 as an inside- or centre-forward, scoring four goals in 21 games. He then moved to Oldham Athletic in 1910 with 50 games and 25 goals. He signed for Bolton in 1911–12 and played 99 games with 28 goals. Bolton won the Manchester Cup during his stay. He was capped by Wales in 1911 and gained seven in total. In 1915 he moved to Swansea and then finished his career in Wales playing again for Aberdare, Pontypridd and Llanbradach.

CONCLUSION AND VIEWS

Bolton Wanderers have enjoyed some success and joy over the years since the 1960s, still influential and a club people wanted to be around. During the 1966 World Cup campaign Brazil used Bolton's facilities and the Bromwich Street training ground, though they had assumed they were going to use Burnden Park, but it was not ready for use in close season. Pele, front left, on the Bromwich Street pitches with team mates.

Unfortunately this once hallowed turf is now a housing estate. Some of the Bolton squad were used to make up numbers for practice and a young John Ritson was chosen as one of the lucky ones. He states it was a pleasure and honour to train with them; they were warm, friendly and passed on their knowledge and skills to the Bolton players.

POST 1960 HONOURS

- Manchester Cup winners: 1960–61 and 1962–63.
- The Third Division title: 1972–73
- League Cup semi-final in 1976–77.
- Second Division title: 1977–78.
- Promotion from Division Four in 1988.
- Losing Finalists in the Freight Rover Trophy 1985–86 to Bristol City 3–0.
- Sherpa Van Trophy winners in 1988–89 beating Torquay United 4–1.
- Lancashire Cup winners in 1988–89, 1–0 and 1990–91, 2–1: both finals against Preston North End. (Competition was sponsored by the Isle of Man). Below is the programme from the 1988–89 Final.

- Promoted from the Second Division in 1992–93.
- League Cup Final 1994–95 with a 2–1 defeat by Liverpool. A great match, which in my humble opinion, the only difference between the two sides being Steve McManaman, some bad luck and an unbelievable save by David James from Alan Thompson. My son Alex was only eight at the time and he can still remember it. In the same year, Bolton was promoted from the First Division into the Premiership with a heart stopping Play-off Final 4–3 win against Reading. The reserves also won the Central League in 1995.
- 2003–4: League Cup Final losing to Middlesbrough 2–1. All the goals coming in the first ten minutes, being two down after seven. A great fight back, but again it was not to be.
- The First Division title in 1996–7.

- Promotion again from Division One/Championship in 2000–01.
- 2005 Premier League Asia Trophy winners and two qualifications for EUFA competitions. Bolton legend Sam Allardyce was in charge from 1999–2007.
- An FA Cup semi-final in 2010–11, but this was the last good run as fortunes declined and they were relegated in 2012.

Bolton Wanderers as a football club, its supporters and the town will always have the ambition and desire to perform at the highest level, which is a tough proposition in a game that is predominantly money driven. A lot of people see this as the downside of football today, but the sad truth is that clubs have now got to look at being a saleable commodity and not just have a good team. You also seem to need the financial backing of someone with what seems to be a bottomless pit of funds.

Any trophies that are gained attempting to achieve any of this are a massive bonus to any club, not just Bolton. They have the foundations to do it and when momentum kicks in with a club like this the fan-base builds very quickly and they get behind their team as well as any other. Some people may not remember or even believe, that in their heyday the road from Farnworth all the way to Burnden Park was a sea of people and the same the other way from the town centre to the ground.

With the right type of backing and structure in place, they may one day climb that ladder right back into their rightful place as a feared top class side. I pray that a turn round in fortunes can be achieved, as this club deserves success again and I know my Aunt is up there somewhere shouting the same message.

I do hope the contents have given you some interest and enjoyment so let's not forget the past of this great club. Hopefully it can assist in igniting the fire and desire required to get Bolton back to where they belong. May it rekindle your enthusiasm for Bolton Wanderers.

THANKS AND DEDICATIONS

I would like to thank my family for their support, encouragement and patience during the time I took putting together this book. Thanks to my Mum and Dad for their imput, passion and knowledge from their time at the club.

My gratitude to Walter and Joyce Sidebottom for their assistance in the collation of information relating to Walter Sidebottom Senior.

Thanks to Simon Marland who gave me information and advice regarding the compilation of the book.

In memory of Elsie Williamson whose love, dedication and enthusiasm for Bolton Wanderers and my family, I am eternally grateful. I think of you every day.

For my cousin Paul Greasley who sadly passed away on 15 May, 2014 aged just 50 years. I miss you pal.

My gratitude to John Ritson for giving up his time to pen his thoughts.

Printed in Germany
by Amazon Distribution
GmbH, Leipzig